Mark's Gospel from Scratch

Also from Westminster John Knox Press by Donald L. Griggs

The Bible from Scratch: The Old Testament for Beginners
The Bible from Scratch: The New Testament for Beginners
Genesis from Scratch: The Old Testament for Beginners (with Gene March, forthcoming)

Mark's Gospel from Scratch

The New Testament for Beginners

Donald L. Griggs
Charles D. Myers Jr.

WJK WESTMINSTER
JOHN KNOX PRESS
LOUISVILLE · KENTUCKY

First edition
Published by Westminster John Knox Press
Louisville, Kentucky

10 11 12 13 14 15 16 17 18 19—10 9 8 7 6 5 4 3 2 1

Book design by Teri Kays Vinson
Cover design by Night & Day Design

Library of Congress Cataloging-in-Publication Data

Griggs, Donald L.
  Mark's Gospel from scratch : the New Testament for beginners /
Donald L. Griggs, Charles D. Myers Jr.
      p. cm.
  Includes bibliographical references.
  ISBN 978-0-664-23486-7 (alk. paper)
  1. Bible. N.T. Mark—Textbooks 2. Bible. N.T. Mark—Commentaries.
I. Myers, Charles Davison. II. Title.
  BS2586.M94 2010
  226.3'07—dc22

                                                                    2009028357

PRINTED IN THE UNITED STATES OF AMERICA

♾ The paper used in this publication meets the minimum requirements of the American National Standard for Information Sciences—Permanence of Paper for Printed Library Materials, ANSI Z39.48-1992

Westminster John Knox Press advocates the responsible use of our natural resources. The text paper of this book is made from 30% post-consumer waste.

Contents

Part One

PARTICIPANT'S GUIDE

CHARLES D. MYERS JR.

Preface to Part One

In the summer of 2008 I was approached at a conference in Virginia by Donald Griggs, well-known Christian educator and author of the popular The Bible from Scratch series on the Old Testament and the New Testament. In light of the success of *The Old Testament for Beginners* and *The New Testament for Beginners*, the editors at Westminster John Knox Press were interested in a follow-up series that would focus attention on individual books of the Bible. Don asked me to collaborate with him on a single book of the Bible, and I readily agreed. As a trained biblical scholar, I agreed to compose the commentary on the work, while Don, an authority on Christian education, would generate questions and exercises that would assist in teaching that particular book. After additional conversations, everyone decided that the Gospel of Mark would be the first book in this new series.

The following study is based on more than twenty years of teaching the Gospel of Mark in college classrooms and in adult education classes in local churches. The audiences I address on a regular basis are interested in increasing their understanding of the Bible, and Mark serves as the perfect entrée into the study of the New Testament. This work, it should be noted, is designed for readers who have little background in the New Testament but who want to learn more about the Bible in general and the Gospel of Mark in particular. My goal is to provide the careful reader with an overall perspective on Mark. To that end, I have tried to avoid technical language and endless commentary. The shortcoming of such an approach is that no topic or text can be considered in too much detail. Perhaps this book will motivate you to consult other books on Mark. I have provided a listing of some such texts.

In order to yield the greatest benefit from this study, I have several suggestions. In the first place, I encourage you to read the text of Mark *before* reading my commentary. The chapters in this book will make more sense if you are familiar with the appropriate biblical material. I also encourage you to follow along in the Bible as you read this text. That technique will also make this study more intelligible. Throughout the text I have included in parentheses many references to Mark and to other pertinent passages in the Bible. These cross-references are intended to make connections with other biblical passages. But the written text should make sense even if you choose not to look up each and every cross-reference.

Another suggestion concerns the English translation that you use in this study. All biblical quotes in this book are taken from the New Revised Standard Version translation that was published in 1989. I am partial to this scholarly translation, because I served as the recording secretary of this project for ten years. My job was to record the changes to the Revised Standard Version text that the translators decided upon, so I had the privilege of watching as this translation was produced. Using the NRSV translation will make it easier to follow this commentary, but any other modern translation of the Bible can be used. I emphasize the notion of *modern* translation, however.

While the King James Version dominated the English-speaking world for more than three centuries, the Greek text of the New Testament on which the KJV translators based their work is a later text than the ones available to translators today. Due to the discovery of many more ancient Greek manuscripts and to refinements in textual criticism in recent years, modern translations of the New Testament are based on more ancient Greek texts than the ones used by the KJV translators. So, for example, the most ancient Greek manuscripts end the Gospel of Mark at 16:8. If there is no mention in the text that Mark 16:9–20 is a later addition to the Gospel, then your translation is not based on the best manuscript evidence available.

One final note: In order to create chapters of equal length, I have divided this study into six chapters. So, for example, after the introductory material in chapter 1, the second chapter covers Mark 1–3, the third chapter covers Mark 4–7, the fourth covers Mark 8–10, the fifth covers Mark 11–14, and the sixth and final chapter covers Mark 15–16. Those divisions, however, are somewhat arbitrary and do not always represent the major transition points in the Gospel.

For that reason I have included an outline of the Gospel that is based more on what I perceive to be the organization of the work. I encourage you to consult that outline frequently.

The Gospel of Mark is my favorite Gospel. After all these years of teaching Mark, I still marvel at the depth and the power of this ancient work. My hope is that *Mark's Gospel from Scratch* will create in you an appreciation for this often-overlooked and underappreciated book of the New Testament.

Gettysburg College
Easter 2009

Chapter One

The Genius of Mark
the Evangelist

An Introduction to the Study of Mark's Gospel

The Relationship of Mark to the Gospels of Matthew and Luke

The Gospel of Mark has not always received the attention that it deserves. Mark is much shorter than the Gospels of Matthew and Luke. Mark lacks much that is familiar to those acquainted with the New Testament, such as birth narratives, genealogies, and resurrection appearances. Mark does not include the Lord's Prayer (Matt. 6:9–13; Luke 11:2–4) or other well-known teachings of Jesus, such as the Beatitudes (Matt. 5:1–12; Luke 6:20–26), the parable of the Good Samaritan (Luke 10:29–37), and the parable of the Sheep and the Goats (Matt. 25:31–46). Moreover, Mark's literary style is less refined than the high literary quality of the Gospels of Matthew and Luke. For all of these reasons, the fuller, more polished Gospels of Matthew and Luke have often overshadowed Mark. This study serves as a corrective to that common approach. As the following study will reveal, Mark's work is a monumental achievement, and the power of Mark's message is not inferior to any other Gospel account.

The modern critical study of Mark is predicated on the scholarly conclusion that *Mark is the earliest of the Gospels in the New Testament.* The current ordering of the four Gospels reflects what the early church thought was their order of composition. Matthew was believed to be the earliest, so it comes first, while John's Gospel was thought to be the latest, so it comes last. From an early time readers have recognized considerable similarities among the first three Gospels. These similarities are even more striking when compared to the distinctly different account in the Fourth Gospel. Matthew, Mark, and Luke share a common overall outline, at times all three Gospels share a common ordering of events, and in some places all three Gospels even share common language. The similarities are so significant that since the early nineteenth century the first three Gospels have been called the Synoptic Gospels, which comes from the Greek word *synopsis*, meaning "view with [the same] eye." The texts of Matthew, Mark, and Luke can be arranged in parallel columns and viewed together in a work called a synopsis or Gospel parallels.

At one time the striking similarities that exist among the first three Gospels were attributed to coincidence. Because the different authors were telling the same story, the overall outline and ordering of events was similar in all three Gospels, or so it was thought. Because the writers were describing the same events, they just happened to use identical language, or so it was believed. Careful comparisons of the texts of Matthew, Mark, and Luke by scholars in the eighteenth and nineteenth centuries called these earlier assumptions into question. The similarities are so striking and so extensive that the only logical explanation is actual literary dependence. That is to say, one or more of the Gospel writers must have copied the work of an earlier author. But who copied whom? The question about the literary relationship that exists among the first three Gospels is called the *Synoptic Problem*, and the solution to the Synoptic Problem would reveal which of the Gospels was the earliest.

By means of careful and detailed comparisons of the texts of the Synoptic Gospels, biblical scholars in the nineteenth century concluded that *Mark's Gospel was the earliest* and that Matthew and Luke knew Mark's work. *Markan priority*, the idea that Mark is the earliest Gospel, explains why about 90 percent of Mark (about 600 verses) appears in Matthew and about 50 percent (some 350 verses) appears in Luke. Fewer than thirty verses of Mark are not found in either Matthew or Luke, and the omission of those verses is rather easy to explain. For example, following the arrest of Jesus in Mark's account we learn that "a certain young man was following [Jesus], wearing nothing but a linen cloth. They caught hold of him, but he left the linen cloth and ran off naked" (14:51–52). This detail of the story was probably not deemed important enough to include in either Matthew or Luke. The other Markan verses (see, for example, 4:26–29; 7:31–37; 8:22–26; 9:49–50) that both Matthew and Luke exclude probably did not suit the narrative needs of the later Evangelists. (Note: I am capitalizing Evangelists when I use the term as a substitute for one or more of four authors of the Gospels. This is in contrast to evangelists [lowercase] who are preachers.)

Markan priority is also demonstrated by those instances when Matthew and Luke "correct" Mark. At the beginning of his Gospel Mark writes, "As it is written in the prophet Isaiah. . ." (1:2a), but he goes on in 1:2b to cite a passage from Malachi: "'See, I am sending my messenger ahead of you, who will prepare your way'" (Mal. 3:1). Not until 1:3 does Mark quote Isaiah: "'the voice of one crying out in the wilderness: "Prepare the way of the Lord, make his paths straight"'" (Isa. 40:3). In the parallel passages, Matthew 3:3 and Luke 3:4, the Malachi quote of Mark 1:2b is simply omitted. By correcting Mark in this manner, Matthew and Luke bear witness to Markan priority.

Markan priority has important implications for how one studies the New Testament. Because Mark is the earliest of the canonical Gospels, the study of the Gospels should begin with Mark. Markan priority also has important implications for how one reads the Gospel of Mark. To understand what Mark has to say one must consider carefully the text of Mark in isolation from the works of Matthew and Luke. This approach is justified historically. Because the Gospels of Matthew and Luke did not exist at the time of the writing of Mark, the author of Mark's Gospel did not assume that Matthew and Luke would supplement his work. The proper approach to this Gospel, therefore, is for the reader to adopt the perspective of the original audience and listen to the message of this Gospel without reference to Matthew and Luke. Appreciating Mark on Mark's own terms will reveal the true genius of Mark the Evangelist.

"The beginning . . ." (1:1a)

The Gospel of Mark opens with these words: "The beginning of the good news of Jesus Christ, the Son of God" (1:1). This initial verse provides vital information for a proper understanding of the work that follows. In the first place, it represents the beginning of this author's work. "The Gospel according to Mark," the current title of the work, was added decades after the completion of this writing. In the second century AD, the work under consideration was attributed to one of Peter's disciples, who is called "my son Mark" in 1 Peter 5:13. Since the traditional title is not a part of the original text of the Gospel, and no one in the body of this work is identified as its actual author, then what is known as the Gospel of Mark is the work of an anonymous author. For the sake of convenience and in keeping with tradition, we will continue to refer to the author of this work as Mark the Evangelist, that is, Mark the Gospel writer. But calling this author "Mark" is a literary convenience. The author's identity remains unknown, which is the way the author must have wanted it to be. After all, the message of Mark's Gospel is much more important than the identity of the author. Besides, this story does not belong to the author. This story belongs to the church.

What, then, is the purpose of this opening verse in general and the meaning of the term "the beginning" in particular? Does this verse simply state that the story about Jesus begins here, that is, with the baptism of Jesus (1:9–11), which is preceded by the introduction of John the Baptist (1:2–8)? Or is Mark 1:1 the superscription or title of the entire work that follows? Note that this verse is not a sentence, for it is missing a verb. Moreover, in ancient literature the first line of a work often functioned as its title. Since the traditional title, "The Gospel according to Mark," is not original, could this initial verse be the title that the author intended the work to have? We will return to this question at the conclusion of our study.

". . . of the gospel . . ." (1:1b)

Mark is the earliest Gospel, having been composed about AD 70, but *Mark is not the earliest writing in the New Testament*. Seven epistles by the Apostle Paul—Romans, 1 and 2 Corinthians, Galatians, Philippians, 1 Thessalonians, and Philemon—were all written in the 50s and, therefore, predate the writing of Mark by some fifteen to twenty years. In these seven writings Paul shows a general lack of interest in the particulars of Jesus' earthly life. At the beginning of 1 Corinthians 15, which Paul wrote in the mid-50s, Paul "remind[s]" the Corinthians of "the gospel" (Gk. *euangelion*) that he "proclaimed" (1 Cor. 15:1) to them when he founded the church in Corinth in the late 40s. Paul then articulates the content of his "gospel" by citing an early Christian creedal statement that summarizes what is "of first importance" (1 Cor. 15:3a), namely, the death and resurrection of Jesus Christ (1 Cor. 15:3b–5). Paul's use of this ancient creed demonstrates that the death and resurrection of Christ were understood as the crucial elements of the "gospel" from the outset of the Christian movement. When Paul uses the term "gospel," he is referring to a short, concise message about God's saving work in Jesus' death and resurrection.

Paul's relative lack of interest in the details of Jesus' earthly life is a function of Paul's belief that a new age had dawned with the death and resurrection of Christ, one that was to be consummated in the near future by Christ's coming (Gk. *parousia*; see 1 Cor. 15:23), as the remaining portion of 1 Corinthians 15 explains (see especially 1 Cor. 15:50–57). For this reason, Paul's interest lay in the present lordship of the risen Christ, not in the past earthly life of Jesus of Nazareth. Paul and the rest of the first generation of Christians were oriented toward the future, not toward the past, and therefore they lacked an interest in history for history's sake.

This does not mean that what Jesus said and did were unimportant in the early Christian movement. On the contrary, from the earliest years the words and deeds of Jesus circulated widely, but these early traditions circulated in oral form as individual units, without time or place references. So a story about Jesus performing a miracle may have been told and then explained in a worship service, or one of Jesus' parables may have been used to teach new converts about the Christian faith. Surely the words and deeds of Jesus were told and retold, but belief in the nearness of the end-time most likely discouraged the first Christians from writing down the details of Jesus' earthly life and teaching in those early years. When faced with the imminent end of the world, it did not occur to Christians to take the time and the trouble to document the past.

If Mark was the first of the Gospels, then Mark was the first one to arrange and order these individual units of oral tradition into a unified, written document. Mark the Evangelist may be seen more as an editor than an author per se. Mark did not create much of the material in the Gospel. Rather, he arranged the material into a unified whole that he called a "gospel" (*euangelion* in 1:1). Mark's use of "gospel," therefore, was a new usage of the term. Whereas the term "gospel" for Paul referred to a succinct message about God's saving work in the death and resurrection of Jesus, for Mark "gospel" describes a type of literature that recounts, in a continuous narrative, the events leading up to and including the death and resurrection of Jesus. The New Revised Standard Version translation of Mark 1:1 renders the Greek *euangelion* as "good news," which is what the term means literally. In Greek *eu-* means "good" and *angelion* means "news." But the more traditional translation of the term *euangelion* as "gospel" better demonstrates that Mark is using this well-known term as a way of identifying a new literary genre.

"... of Jesus Christ, the Son of God" (1:1c)

Although Mark is the earliest Gospel, it is not an "objective" biography that treats the life and times of Jesus of Nazareth in strict chronological order. Mark was composed before the Gospels of Matthew, Luke, and John, to be sure, but Mark is not a purely objective account of Jesus' life, one uninfluenced by theological concerns. That is evident from the end of Mark 1:1, which concludes with the words "of Jesus Christ, the Son of God." Some ancient Greek manuscripts omit the phrase "the Son of God" in 1:1. But the sources that do so are later than those sources that include the phrase, so the original reading of this verse must have contained "the Son of God."

By identifying Jesus as the "Christ, the Son of God," the author confirms that what follows is not a neutral account of the life and times of Jesus of Nazareth. The first verse assumes that Jesus is the "Christ, the Son of God," so the author must assume from the outset that the audience also accepts this. Mark's Gospel, therefore, is written *by* a person of faith *to* persons of faith. Furthermore, the readers know Jesus' true identity from the very beginning of the work. What the readers know, as we shall see, contrasts significantly with what the characters in the narrative know.

Other aspects of Mark's narrative prove that Mark's primary interest was not in providing a historically accurate, day-by-day account of the life and times of Jesus. In other words, Mark is not a biography in the strict sense of the word, and this is evident when one considers what Mark lacks. For example, Mark's treatment of the life of Jesus is incomplete. There is nothing in Mark about the early years of Jesus' life. In Mark's Gospel we first encounter Jesus at his baptism, when he is an adult. Although Mark focuses attention on the public ministry of Jesus, not everything that Jesus said and did is included. The selective treatment of the life of the main character is not characteristic of a biography.

Mark also omits other elements that characterize biographies. Most notably, Mark says nothing about Jesus' outward appearance. What biography does not have some description of the physical appearance of the main character? Mark also provides no details about Jesus' inner thoughts or about his personal development. Jesus appears on the scene as a fully mature character, and he changes very little as the story advances. This, too, is unusual for a biography, which usually treats in great depth the emotional and intellectual development of the subject of the work.

Mark also exhibits little interest in providing a sequentially accurate chronology of Jesus' life. To be sure, Mark's Gospel has an overall chronological outline that moves from baptism to public ministry to death and resurrection. But Mark seems relatively unconcerned with the exact timing of particular events. Specific time references, for instance, are relatively infrequent in Mark's Gospel. In 4:35 Jesus and the disciples set out "on that day, when evening had come," but the next explicit chronological reference does not occur until 6:2, where it simply says "on the sabbath." Many incidents are simply introduced by the author's favorite time reference, "and immediately" (Gk. *kai euthus*), which appears some forty-two times in the Greek text of Mark. These abrupt transitions give Mark's Gospel the feel of a slideshow that moves rapidly from scene to scene. Matthew and Luke, with their more fluid transitions between scenes, turn Mark's slideshow into a motion picture.

Evidently, Mark's primary interest was not to provide a historically accurate, sequential account of Jesus' earthly life. This is not surprising, however, for the early church in general lacked such a purely historical interest. Besides, Mark's Gospel was written some forty years after the death of Jesus, so the author's sources of information may have been limited. Moreover, the nature of the oral tradition may have made the historical reconstruction of Jesus' life difficult. The units of oral tradition contain few clues about their relation to other events. Jesus' words and deeds are often introduced in the most general terms, such as "One sabbath he was going through the grainfields" (2:23a). This bit of tradition circulated without any indications about *where* the grainfield was located, *when* this incident occurred during his public ministry, or *how* this incident relates to other events in Jesus' ministry.

If Mark was the first Gospel, and prior to Mark the material about Jesus circulated orally as individual units of tradition, then Mark was the first one to arrange those bits of oral tradition in a particular order. By arranging, altering, and augmenting the individual units of tradition, Mark made those individual units serve an overall interpretation of the earthly career of Jesus. But historical accuracy was not what informed Mark's arrangement of these units of oral tradition. Mark's primary concern was theological, not historical. The author used these elements of tradition in order to make a theological statement about who the risen Lord is and what it means to be his follower. Therefore, even the earliest of the Gospels is not an objective, historical account of the earthly life of Jesus.

As the earliest of the canonical Gospels, however, Mark represents a remarkable display of creativity. Having created a new type of Christian writing called a "gospel," the writer did something that no one else in the early church had ever done. The very fact that we cannot envision a New Testament without Gospels attests to the overwhelming success of his literary experiment. But if Mark's primary concern was not historical accuracy, then we must listen carefully to his distinctive message. In subsequent chapters we will explore the distinctive message of Mark's Gospel and come to an even greater appreciation of the genius of Mark the Evangelist.

Chapter Two

The Beginning of the Gospel

A Study of Mark 1:1–3:35

The Structure of the Gospel of Mark

Central to the Gospel is Mark's portrayal of Jesus Christ, and on the basis of this portrayal, the Gospel can be neatly divided into two halves. The first half of Mark (1:14–8:30) portrays Jesus as a highly successful and astonishingly popular wonder worker. The vast majority of Jesus' miraculous works are concentrated in the first eight chapters, where he performs eleven healings and four nature miracles. Jesus also silences all spiritual and earthly opposition by his powerful word and deed. Moreover, Jesus' popularity is tremendous. He attracts great crowds of people from all over. In the first half of the Gospel, Mark portrays Jesus as *the powerful Christ*.

The second half of the Gospel (8:31–15:47), however, is dominated by the cross and the events leading up to Jesus' death. Here Jesus' miraculous works diminish greatly. In this part of Mark, Jesus performs only two healings and one nature miracle. His popularity dwindles, and his opponents appear to gain the upper hand, because they succeed in arresting him, trying him, and handing him over to the authorities to be put to death. In the second half of the Gospel, Mark portrays Jesus as *the suffering Christ.*

These two halves are framed by the prologue (1:1–13), which covers the events prior to the initiation of Jesus' public ministry, and the epilogue (16:1–8), which describes the scene at the empty tomb. In this chapter we will consider the prologue (1:1–13) and the initial phase of Jesus' public ministry in Galilee (1:14–3:35).

The Prologue of Mark's Gospel (1:1–13)

Mark's use of the term "gospel" in 1:1 describes a new type of literature that is characterized by a sequential narrative of the events leading up to and including the death and resurrection of Jesus Christ. The gospel as a type of literature was not an obvious literary option in the early church. The epistle was the earliest, most basic, and most widely used literary form in the early church. The fact that the New Testament contains twenty-one epistles, some of which predate Mark, attests to that fact. The gospel as a literary form represented an innovation in early Christian literature. As the writer of the earliest of the canonical Gospels, Mark was the inventor of this form.

In Mark's Gospel Jesus first appears on the scene at his baptism (1:9–10). Missing from Mark are the annunciation, the birth, and the genealogy of Jesus, as well as any treatment of his infancy, childhood, or youth. In Mark, Jesus bursts on the scene as an adult, with only some minor references to his familial background elsewhere in the Gospel (3:21, 31; 6:3).

Before Jesus can be baptized, however, John the Baptist needs to be introduced (1:2–8). Although the author misidentifies the Malachi quote of 1:2b as coming from Isaiah (1:2a), this quote and other references in Mark 1 serve to portray John as the *forerunner* of Jesus. The Malachi passage mentions a "messenger" that is sent by God "'ahead . . . who will prepare . . .'" (1:2b), then the Isaiah passage refers to "the voice of one crying out in the wilderness, 'Prepare the way of the Lord'" (1:3). When John is described as living in the wilderness (1:4), the reader sees the immediate connection between these verses and the role of John. In John's subsequent preaching he mentions that one "'more powerful than I is coming after me'" (1:7). And John as forerunner is further expressed in the comment in Mark 1:14a that mentions the imprisonment of John just prior to the beginning of Jesus' public ministry. Although John's death at the hands of Herod Antipas is not described until Mark 6:14–29, the forerunner must exit the scene before the main character enters. Because we recognize John as the forerunner, the one who "'prepare[s] the way of the Lord,'" John the Baptist's preparatory activity in Mark confirms that Jesus is "'the [coming] Lord,'" even before Jesus appears in the story.

John baptizes Jesus in Mark 1:9, but there is no indication in the text that John recognizes who Jesus is, either before or after Jesus' baptism. During Jesus' baptism Mark explains that "he saw the heavens torn apart and the Spirit descending like a dove on him" (1:10), which suggests that only Jesus sees the heavens opened and the Spirit descend. Then a voice from heaven says, "'You are my Son, the Beloved; with you I am well pleased'" (1:11). Here the voice addresses Jesus directly ("'You are. . .'"), and there is no indication that others overheard what was said. Mark's account is unique when compared to the later Gospel accounts. In Matthew's version the heavenly voice addresses John (and presumably anyone else within earshot) when it testifies, "'This is my Son . . .'" (Matt. 3:17), and in Luke's account everyone present witnesses the coming of the Spirit, because it descends "in bodily form like a dove" (Luke 3:22). In Mark's Gospel, however, after Jesus' baptism only God, the Spirit, Jesus, and the reader know Jesus' true identity.

What God says at Jesus' baptism in Mark provides an important clue about Jesus' identity. The words spoken from heaven are composed of two biblical quotes. The first part, "'You are my Son, the Beloved'" (1:11a), comes from Psalm 2, which is a royal psalm and describes what happens on the day that the new king ascends to the throne of Israel. Kings were anointed on the day they became king in ancient Israel, beginning with Saul (see 1 Sam. 10:1). For this reason a synonym for king is "anointed one." The Hebrew term for "anointed one" is *meshiah*, from which we get the term "messiah." Psalm 2, which speaks about "the LORD and his anointed" (Ps. 2:2b), goes on to say, "[The Lord] said to me, 'You are my son; today I have begotten you'" (Ps. 2:7b). On the day of the new king's ascension to the throne, the king is "adopted" as the Son of God. One sign of that adoption is possession of the Holy Spirit. So, for example, on the day that he was anointed king of Israel "the spirit of the LORD came mightily upon David from that day forward" (1 Sam. 16:13). Through the baptismal event Jesus is anointed "Son of God" and from that time henceforth is possessed by the Holy Spirit. Mark shows no interest in the life of Jesus prior to his baptism because the real story begins with his baptism!

But there is a second part to the words that the divine voice speaks to Jesus, and these words—"'with you I am well pleased'" (1:11b)—come from Isaiah 42:1. A distinctive feature of this portion of Isaiah is the presence of four so-called Servant Songs (42:1–4; 49:1–6; 50:4–9; 52:13–53:12), which describe one who suffers on behalf of others. Who is the Servant that is described? While the Servant in these chapters appears at times to be the nation of Israel (see Isa. 49:3; see also 41:8–10; 43:8–13; 44:1–2, 21; 45:4; 48:20), the Servant Songs also depict the Suffering Servant as an individual (see Isa. 49:1–2, 4–6; see also 42:1–4; 50:4–11; 52:13–53:12). Isaiah 42:1, which is spoken by God at Jesus' baptism, is the first verse of the first Servant Song. Mark (and others in the early Christian church) saw in Isaiah 42:1 and in the other Servant Songs a reference to Jesus. By citing Isaiah 42:1 at Jesus' baptism (1:11b), therefore, God intimates that the newly "anointed one" is destined to suffer on behalf of others.

As soon as Jesus receives the Spirit at his baptism the Spirit casts Jesus out into the wilderness, where he is brought into conflict with the spiritual powers (1:12–13). As the bearer of God's Spirit, Jesus will not only contend with human opposition but will also encounter spiritual opposition. In this passage Jesus' opponent is Satan; later it will be unclean spirits and demons. The reference to Jesus being "in the wilderness forty days" (1:13a) recalls the forty-year period of wandering in the wilderness that Israel endured after the exodus event. Unlike Israel, Jesus remains faithful during his time of trial and temptation. Jesus has the power of God on his side, as represented by the angels that "waited on him" (1:13b). In the prologue of Mark, then, Jesus is called by God, armed with the power of the Holy Spirit, and tested by Satan himself. Jesus is now ready to begin his public ministry.

The First Phase of Jesus' Public Ministry (1:14–3:35)

Jesus' public ministry begins in the northern province of Galilee "after John was arrested" (1:14a). Jesus comes "proclaiming the gospel [Gk. *euangelion*] of God" (1:14). Here the "gospel" that Jesus preaches is described as "'The time is fulfilled, and the kingdom of God has come near; repent, and believe in the gospel'" (1:15). Unlike Mark's use of the term "gospel" in 1:1, in these two later verses in the same chapter the term "gospel" is used in its more traditional sense to mean a concise statement about God's saving activity that can be preached.

In the first half of Mark's Gospel Jesus is portrayed as a person powerful in word and deed. That power is evidenced from the start of his public ministry, when he calls his first disciples (1:16–20). Jesus does not introduce himself to Simon and Andrew or to James and John. When Jesus calls, people respond "immediately" (1:18, 20), without asking any questions and after being told only that Jesus will "'make [them] fish for people'" (1:17). The immediate and unquestioning response of the first disciples to the call of Jesus proves the power of Jesus' word.

Jesus' power is demonstrated further in the miracles that he performs. He heals three specific individuals and some unspecified persons (1:34, 39) all in the first chapter of Mark's Gospel. Jesus first heals a man with an unclean spirit (1:21–28) who appears in the synagogue in Capernaum on the Sabbath. Now the unclean spirits recognize Jesus, for this spirit cries out, "'I know who you are, the Holy One of God'" (1:24b). There is no indication in the text, however, that anyone but Jesus hears what the spirit says. Jesus immediately rebukes the spirit by saying, "'Be silent, and come out of him!'" (1:25).

Jesus' curious command to the unclean spirit to "'be silent!'" represents the first component of a distinctive theme in Mark called the *messianic secret motif*. On many occasions in Mark's Gospel Jesus demands that his identity not be revealed. Later in the same chapter we learn that Jesus "would not permit the demons to speak, because they knew him" (1:34b). The crowd reacts to Jesus' exorcism with amazement (1:27), while "his fame began to spread throughout the surrounding region of Galilee" (1:28).

Jesus then heals Simon's mother-in-law, who is suffering from a fever (1:29–31). After healing others in Capernaum (1:32–34), Jesus preaches and heals elsewhere in Galilee (1:35–39). He then cleanses a leper (1:40–45), which is his third miraculous healing in Mark 1. Two details of the story are noteworthy. The first is that Jesus touches this untouchable (1:41). In a society that segregated lepers from the rest of the population because of the contagion of their dreaded disease, Jesus touches the man to heal him. Elsewhere Jesus heals by means of his powerful word (see 1:21–28; 2:1–12; 3:1–6; 5:1–13; 9:14–29; 10:46–52) without any physical contact, but Jesus' power is demonstrated in his touching the leprous man while not contracting the disease. The second point is that this skin disease leaves the man's body "immediately" (1:42), which is a further demonstration of Jesus' power. Skin diseases never heal "immediately," even with modern scientific advances. This one does.

Afterward, Jesus "sternly" charges the man to say nothing about the healing (1:43–44). Here is a second component of the messianic secret motif: Jesus commands those healed (and those who witness) to keep silent. The man, however, disobeys Jesus and tells everyone (1:45a), with the result that Jesus "could no longer go into a town openly" (1:45b). Jesus' fame does not help his ministry. In fact, it hinders his work. By the end of the first chapter in Mark's Gospel, therefore, Jesus is seen as powerful in word and deed and immensely popular with the people.

Chapters 2 and 3 introduce a new element into the story, namely, opposition, which comes in the form of controversy with the religious leaders over the healing of the paralytic, the next miracle that Jesus performs (2:1–12). This story attests to Jesus' popularity, because four persons carrying the paralytic man cannot get near to Jesus in his house in Capernaum, so they "removed the roof above him . . . and let down the mat on which the paralytic lay" (2:4). Rather than heal the paralytic immediately, Jesus first says, "'Son, your sins are forgiven'" (2:5). This remark incenses the Jewish scribes, for they reason, "'Who can forgive sins but God alone?'" (2:7b). By healing the paralytic, however, Jesus proves not only his power to heal but also his "authority on earth to forgive sins" (2:10).

Controversy continues after Jesus calls a tax collector named Levi (2:13–14) then dines with Levi and his friends (2:15–17). The "scribes of the Pharisees" rebuke Jesus for eating with sinners (2:16), but Jesus silences his opposition with the statement "'Those who are well have no need of a physician, but those who are sick; I have come to call not the righteous but sinners'" (2:17). Related to the topic of eating practices is the topic of fasting. Jesus is challenged by those who say that "'John's disciples and the Pharisees'" fast, while Jesus' disciples do not. Jesus responds that now is not the time to fast, for "'the bridegroom is with them'" (2:19). Fasting will be more appropriate at a later time (2:20).

After two stories dealing with problems related to eating (2:13–22) come two stories related to Sabbath observance (2:23–3:6). The first involves Jesus and his disciples walking through a grainfield on the Sabbath (2:23–2). When the Pharisees criticize Jesus' disciples for plucking "heads of grain" in violation of the commandment that prohibits any work on the Sabbath (Exod. 20:8–11; Deut. 5:12–15), Jesus silences his opponents with his powerful word, "'The sabbath was made for humankind, and not humankind for the sabbath'" (2:27).

Then Jesus heals a man with a withered hand on the Sabbath (3:1–5), which is another supposed violation of the law of Moses. Jesus challenges the Pharisaic interpretation of the Sabbath command by asking if "doing good" on the Sabbath is permitted, for healing is a form of "doing good." The Pharisees are silent. Angry and grieved at the hard-hearted Pharisaic interpretation of the Law (3:3–5a), Jesus defies the Pharisees by healing the man with the withered hand (3:5b). The result of this miracle is that "the Pharisees went out and immediately conspired with the Herodians against him, how to destroy him" (3:6).

In spite of the growing opposition on the part of the religious leaders, Jesus' popularity continues to grow. Jesus' appeal has considerable geographical reach, even beyond Israel's borders (3:8). But his popularity threatens his well-being. The throngs of people are so great and the desire to touch him so overwhelming that Jesus has to take evasive action in order to avoid being crushed (3:9). And while the unclean spirits know that he is "'the Son of God'" (3:11), the crowds apparently do not. They hear about this great wonder worker and travel miles to see him in action, but there is no indication that these throngs know Jesus' true identity. In keeping with the messianic secret motif, Jesus silences the unclean spirits, because they know who he is (3:12). The fact that Jesus does not need to silence the crowds confirms their ignorance of his identity.

After appointing the Twelve (3:13–19a), the first phase of Jesus' ministry concludes with a visit to his home (3:19b). In light of all that Jesus has said and done to date, surely people now know who Jesus is. Most certainly one would expect Jesus' own family and the religious scholars of the day to be the most aware. But when Jesus returns home the members of his family "went out to restrain him," because they questioned his sanity (3:21). In other words, his own family attempts to keep Jesus from his work. Additionally, "the scribes who came down from Jerusalem" (3:22a), the most learned scholars of the day, question Jesus' authority. Rather than being filled with the Holy Spirit, they think that he is allied with the forces of evil (3:22b) and possessed by an unclean spirit (3:30).

Jesus first rebuts the scribes, who charge that his power comes from Satan. "'How can Satan cast out Satan?'" he asks (3:23b). If Satan is casting out Satan, reasons Jesus, then "'his end has come'" (3:26). In reaction to their disbelief in him (3:21) Jesus snubs his own family when they ask to see him (3:31). Note that "his mother and his brothers" are depicted as "standing outside" (3:31b, 32b) when they make their request. They are not a part of the "crowd [that] was sitting around him" (3:32a, 34a). They are not a part of his inner circle of believers. The true relatives of Jesus are those who do the will of God, and Jesus' birth family does not meet that standard (3:35).

Therefore, the initial phase of Jesus' ministry is a clear testimony to the reader of who Jesus is, but it only serves to confuse the characters in the story. Even after he has performed five miracles and has silenced all human and spiritual opposition, people still do not know who Jesus is. Rather than clarifying his identity, the miracles of Jesus seem to cloud his identity. He is popular, to be sure, but he is popular because he works wonders. Even those who should know who he is—his family and the most highly trained scholars of the day—fail to grasp his true identity. The only ones who know who Jesus truly is are God, Jesus, the Holy Spirit and the angels, Satan and the evil spirits—and the readers of Mark's Gospel! The other characters in the story remain clueless.

Chapter Three

Jesus the Wonder Worker

A Study of Mark 4:1–7:37

In the first three chapters of Mark, Jesus has shown himself to be powerful in word and deed. He has silenced demons who know his identity (1:25, 34b; 3:12) as well as his human opponents who do not know who he is (2:8–12, 17, 19–22, 25–28; 3:4–5). The power of his word has also been seen in his calling of his first disciples (1:16–20) and the calling of Levi (2:13–14), all of whom follow Jesus without question. Jesus' powerful deeds in this portion of the Gospel include five impressive miracles that are described in some detail—casting out an evil spirit (1:21–28), healing Simon's mother-in-law (1:29–31), cleansing a leper (1:40–45), healing a paralytic (2:1–12), and healing a man with a withered hand (3:1–6)—in addition to healings that are mentioned but not described (1:34, 39; 3:10–11). But when Jesus goes home, his own family thinks he is crazy (3:21), and the scribes from Jerusalem think he is demon possessed (3:30). While the miracles have attracted crowds of people, Jesus' miraculous works have not revealed his true identity.

Jesus Teaches in Parables (4:1–34)

Chapter 4 provides a brief interlude before the onset of the second phase of Jesus' public ministry. Here Jesus teaches in parables. Most of the parables in Mark are concentrated in this chapter, with the notable exception of the parable of the Wicked Tenants (12:1–12). Parables, which are extended metaphors built on events and experiences from daily life, are used to describe the indescribable, such as the kingdom of God. Often they include an introductory phrase such as "The kingdom of God is like . . ." A true parable has a single point of comparison. The parable of the Mustard Seed (4:30–32) is a genuine parable, for it simply contrasts insignificant beginnings with significant endings.

The chapter begins with Jesus seated in a boat on the Sea of Galilee teaching "a very large crowd" (4:1) on shore. He starts "to teach them many things in parables" (4:2a), beginning with the parable of the Sower (4:3–9). Later, when Jesus is alone with his inner circle of followers, he comments, "'To you has been given the secret of the kingdom of God, but for those outside, everything comes in parables'" (4:11). Here is the distinction between those inside and those "outside" that was seen in the prior passage about Jesus and his family (3:31–35). Quoting a passage from the call of the prophet Isaiah (Isa. 6:10b), Jesus says that he speaks in parables so that those outside "'"may indeed look, but not perceive, and may indeed listen, but not understand; so that they may not turn again and be forgiven"'" (4:12). The parables, therefore, are intended to confound "those outside."

Those inside, on the other hand, have been given "the secret of the kingdom of God" (4:11a), because Jesus explains the parables to the insiders, as he does with the parable of the Sower (4:3–9). But Jesus' interpretation here (4:14–20) is allegorical, for each detail of the story signifies something else. Thus the seed is "the word" (4:14), the birds (4:4) represent Satan (4:15b), and the various types of soil represent various responses to "the word." Moreover, "the sun" (4:6) refers to "trouble or persecution [that] arises on account of the word" (4:17), and the "thorns" (4:7) are "the cares of the world, and the lure of wealth, and the desire for other things [that] come in and choke the word" (4:19). In these verses Jesus practices what is later stated, namely, that Jesus "did not speak to them except in parables, but he explained everything in private to his disciples" (4:34). Now the disciples have the inside track. They have greater knowledge than others in the narrative, for Jesus explains the meaning of what he says publicly to his disciples "in private" (4:34).

The Second Phase of Jesus' Public Ministry (4:35–6:6a)

After this brief teaching interlude, Jesus sets out on the second phase of his public ministry. In this phase he is portrayed as a superlative miracle worker.

Jesus performed five impressive miracles in the first phase, but the four miracles he performs in this second phase are even bigger and better. Jesus' first miracle in this section shows his power over nature (4:35–41). Although "a great windstorm arose [on the Sea of Galilee], and the waves beat into the boat, so that the boat was already being swamped" (4:37), Jesus is found "in the stern, asleep on the cushion" (4:38a). His disciples, who are frantic and fearful for their very lives, awaken Jesus. Mark records that Jesus simply "rebuked the wind, and said to the sea, 'Peace! Be still!'" (4:39a). The result of Jesus' spoken word is "a dead calm" (4:39b). Jesus' word silences the chaos of creation! But Jesus' subsequent question is telling: "'Why are you afraid? Have you still no faith?'" (4:40) he asks the disciples. Though "they were filled with great awe," they still wondered, "'Who then is this, that even the wind and the sea obey him?'" (4:41b). Apparently, the disciples still do not know Jesus' true identity.

Jesus' next miracle is an exorcism, the most common form of miracle that Jesus has performed to date in the Gospel (see 1:21–28, 34, 39; 3:11). But the Gerasene demoniac that Jesus encounters in Mark 5 is not your average demoniac. This man was an outcast who "lived among the tombs" (5:3), was too strong to be restrained by anyone or anything (5:4), and was "always howling and bruising himself with stones" (5:5). Of course, the demon recognizes Jesus as "Son of the Most High God" as soon as they meet (5:7). But when Jesus learns that this man is possessed by about two thousand unclean spirits, he casts them out of the man and allows them to enter a nearby herd of swine (5:13). After the Gerasene man is cleansed, he begs Jesus to allow him to follow (5:18), but Jesus does not give him permission (5:19a). Instead Jesus instructs the man, "'Go home to your friends, and tell them how much *the Lord* has done for you, and what mercy he has shown you'" (5:19b; italics mine). But we learn in the next verse that "he went away and began to proclaim in the Decapolis how much *Jesus* had done for him" (5:20; italics mine). The man does not do what Jesus commands, even though the reader knows from chapter 1 that Jesus is the Lord whose way was prepared by John.

Jesus' next miracle involves a healing (5:24b–34) that is framed by the story of the raising of Jairus's daughter from the dead (5:21–24a, 35–43). A leader of the synagogue, Jairus by name, throws himself at Jesus' feet and begs Jesus to lay hands on his daughter who "'is at the point of death'" (5:23). Jesus is on his way to Jairus's home when something remarkable happens.

The story of the healing of the hemorrhaging woman begins with the reference to the crowd around Jesus that "pressed in on him" (5:24b). Then the condition of the ailing woman is provided in great detail. She has been suffering from hemorrhages for twelve years (5:25). Moreover, she has spent all of her money on ineffective medical treatments, so now she is broke and still sick (5:26). Having "heard about Jesus" (5:27), the woman pushes her way through the dense crowd in a valiant attempt to touch Jesus' cloak. Upon touching his garment, "immediately her hemorrhage stopped" (5:29). Jesus is so powerful that his very clothes can heal people!

Although he did not see her, Jesus senses "that power had gone forth from him" (5:30a), so he stops and asks, "'Who touched my clothes?'" (5:30b). In light of the throngs of people, the disciples find Jesus' question highly inappropriate, and they tell him so: "'You see the crowd pressing in on you; how can you say, "Who touched me?"'" (5:31). But Jesus is undeterred. He looks around and finds the newly healed woman, who reports to Jesus "the whole truth" (5:33). The contrast between the faith of the woman, who had never even seen Jesus before this incident, and the faith of the disciples, who were "insiders," is striking. The disciples still lack understanding.

This encounter with the hemorrhaging woman delays Jesus just long enough for Jairus's daughter to die. When news of her death arrives (5:35), Jesus tells Jairus, "'Do not fear, only believe'" (5:36b). Peter, James, and John accompany Jesus to Jairus's house, where the family and friends are in the throes of grief. Jesus enters the home and announces, "'The child is not dead but sleeping'" (5:39b). So stunned are the mourners at the outrageous declaration of Jesus that "they laughed at him" (5:40a). But taking his three disciples along with Jairus and his wife, Jesus enters the room where the child was laid out and raises her from the dead (5:41–42a). All were "overcome with amazement" (5:42b), but Jesus "strictly ordered them that no one should know this" (5:43).

Now, after performing four supermiracles—stilling a storm, casting out two thousand demons, healing a woman who merely touches his clothes, and raising a little girl from the dead—Jesus returns to his hometown (6:1) only to find that people still do not know who he is (6:2–3a). Rather than welcoming him with open arms, the people of his hometown "took offense at him" (6:3b). The miracles of Jesus cloud rather than clarify Jesus' identity. This phase of Jesus' public ministry ends with the comment that Jesus "was amazed at their unbelief" (6:6a). Whereas others have been "amazed" at Jesus' works (5:20; see also 1:27; 2:12; 5:42), Jesus is now "amazed" at how he is being received. And those who have known him the longest—those from his hometown, his own relatives, and members of his household—seem to be the most skeptical about him. Their lack of faith in him seriously inhibits his ability to heal or do any "deed of power" (6:5) in his hometown, so he travels elsewhere (6:6b).

Perhaps after two phases of public ministry (1:14–3:35; 4:1–6:6a) Jesus decides that he needs additional workers in the field. For that reason he sends out the Twelve in pairs (6:7). The pairing of disciples may be motivated by the biblical belief that two witnesses were needed to testify to the truth of a matter (Deut. 19:15). While the disciples are away on their mission, Mark narrates the story of the death of John the Baptist (6:14–29). Mark introduces the story of John's death by noting that Herod Antipas learned about Jesus' ministry and believed that Jesus was "'John, whom I beheaded'" (6:16) raised from the dead. This leads to the story of how John died.

John the Baptist was critical of Herod's marriage to Herodias, who was once married to Herod's brother Philip. Herod Antipas arrested John but was afraid to do more to him, because Herod knew that John "was a righteous and holy man" (6:20). Herodias had no such qualms, however. On Herod's birthday, when the daughter of Herodias danced to the delight of Herod, Herod granted her one request (6:21–23). After consulting with her mother Herodias, the daughter asked for "'the head of John the Baptist on a platter'" (6:25b). Herod obliged. John was immediately beheaded, and the head was presented to the daughter and Herodias (6:27–28). John's disciples then claimed John's body and buried it in a tomb (6:29).

The story of John's death foreshadows the death of Jesus. John is portrayed in Mark (1:2–8, 14a) as the forerunner of Jesus in life. Now John is portrayed as the forerunner of Jesus in death. It is not coincidental that John is innocent of any real crime, that a Roman official orders the death, and that the official who ordered the execution felt a degree of social pressure in making that decision. In the case of John, Herod acted "out of regard for his oaths and for the guests" (6:26b). In the case of Jesus, Pilate "wishing to satisfy the crowd" (15:15a) sends Jesus to his death.

The Third Phase of Jesus' Public Ministry: First Cycle (6:30–7:37)

The third phase of Jesus' public ministry begins in 6:30, when the disciples return to Jesus from their missionary journeys. Jesus tries to take his disciples away "to a deserted place" for a little rest and relaxation, because the demands of the crowds were exhausting (6:31). But even their attempt to get away by boat for a time is thwarted, for crowds follow them and arrive at their landing site ahead of them (6:32–33).

Mark says that when Jesus "went ashore, he saw a great crowd," so "he began to teach them" (6:34). When the hour grows late, the disciples want Jesus to dismiss the crowd so that people will be able to purchase food for themselves (6:35). Jesus tells the disciples, "'You give them something to eat'" (6:37). The disciples balk at the suggestion, but Jesus takes five loaves of bread and two fish, then blesses and breaks the loaves and gives them to his disciples (6:41). In this nature miracle Jesus feeds "five thousand men" (6:44), and there are still "twelve baskets full of broken pieces and of the fish" (6:43) left over.

After Jesus feeds the multitude, the disciples get into the boat and set out for the other side of the Sea of Galilee, while Jesus stays behind to pray (6:45–46). Early in the morning he performs another nature miracle by walking on the water. Although he "intended to pass them by" (6:48b), when Jesus sees how "they were straining at the oars against an adverse wind" (6:48a) and recognizes how frightened the disciples are at the sight of him coming toward them on the water, he decides to get into the boat with the disciples (6:51a). The story concludes with the comment that the disciples "were utterly astounded, for they did not understand about the loaves, but their hearts were hardened" (6:51b–52). After witnessing two remarkable nature miracles, the disciples remain uncertain about Jesus' true identity.

What follows in Mark 6:53–56 is a short summary paragraph that reveals Jesus' popularity. People from all over were bringing their sick to Jesus, wherever he happened to be. And the very fringe of his cloak had the power to heal anyone who touched it, as we saw earlier in the healing of the hemorrhaging woman (5:25–34). Jesus continues to be seen as a popular and powerful wonder worker.

After the two previous nature miracles, Jesus debates with some Pharisees over "the tradition of the elders" (7:1–23). The tradition that is the subject of this debate is the so-called oral law that developed over many years in Pharisaic circles. The Mosaic law was not always specific enough in its application. For example, the commandment that requires one to "remember the sabbath day, and keep it holy" (Exod. 20:8–11; Deut. 5:12–15) prohibits work on the seventh day but fails to define what constitutes work. Pharisaic leaders called rabbis debated the finer points of the law, and their conclusions composed the oral law. The oral law was organized into six "books" and written down in about AD 200 in a document called the Mishnah. At the time of Jesus, however, "the tradition" was still oral. Jesus has already been critical of the Pharisees' oral law. His disputes with the Pharisees over Sabbath observance (2:23–28; 3:1–6) were challenges to the Pharisees' "tradition of the elders."

The passage begins with the Pharisees criticizing Jesus for some of his disciples "eating with defiled hands" (7:2, 5). The fact that the author has to explain Jewish purity regulations in a parenthetical comment (7:3–4) proves that the audience of this Gospel is Gentile. Jesus responds to this criticism by saying that the Pharisees "abandon the commandment of God and hold to human tradition" (7:8), for they allow the oral law to trump the written law. Jesus gives the example of how the Pharisees get around the commandment to "honor your father and your mother" (Exod. 20:12; Mark 7:10). Contrary to popular understanding, this commandment is addressed to adult "children" who are required to take care of their parents in their old age. The oral tradition allows an adult "child" to identify personal resources as "Corban," which means that they are devoted to God and cannot be used to support one's elderly parents (7:11–12). Jesus criticizes the Pharisees who "'make void the word of God through your [oral] tradition that you have handed on'" (7:13).

Jesus then addresses the crowd about the Pharisaic dietary laws. He argues that "'there is nothing outside a person that by going in can defile, but the things that come out are what defile'" (7:15). As before (4:34), Jesus explains this comment to his disciples when he enters the house (7:17). But Jesus first criticizes the disciples, saying, "'Then do you also fail to understand?'" (7:18a), before he goes on to explain his radical notion that what comes out of the mouth defiles far more than what goes in the mouth (7:20–23).

The next story concerns Jesus' healing of the daughter of a Syrophoenician woman (7:24–30). But this account is more than a simple healing. In the first place, we are told that Jesus departs on the sly for "the region of Tyre" (7:24a), which is in the southern area of modern-day Lebanon. But even in this distant land Jesus "could not escape notice" (7:24b). A woman with a "little daughter [who] had an unclean spirit" (7:25) seeks him out when she learns that he is in the area. This woman, who is the first Gentile that Jesus encounters (7:26a), asks Jesus to cast out the demon from her daughter (7:26b). Jesus responds with the off-putting words, "'Let the children be fed first, for it is not fair to take the children's bread and throw it to the dogs'" (7:27). Of course, the children in this statement are the Jews, and the dogs are the Gentiles. The woman is not offended by Jesus' response. Instead, she replies, "'Sir, even the dogs under the table eat the children's crumbs'" (7:28). In other words, once the Jews have eaten their fill, the Gentiles should have access to the leftovers. Jesus commends the woman for her response, and the woman's reward is the exorcism of her daughter (7:29–30). Although this story is a healing, the focus of the passage is on the discussion between Jesus and the Syrophoenician woman concerning "the children's bread" (rendered "food" in the NRSV).

The final miracle that Jesus performs in this initial cycle (6:30–7:37) of his third phase of public ministry is the healing of a man who is deaf and who suffers from a speech impediment (7:31–37). Jesus "put his fingers into his ears, and he spat and touched his tongue" (7:33).Then, after Jesus looks heavenward and speaks to the man, "immediately his ears were opened, his tongue was released, and he spoke plainly" (7:35). Of course, Jesus told the man and those who witnessed the healing not to tell anyone about it (7:36a). But in a statement that summarizes the all-too-frequent response of people to Jesus' commands, Mark informs us that "the more [Jesus] ordered them [to keep silent], the more zealously they proclaimed it" (7:36b). Then, in a verse that summarizes Jesus' work to date, the author informs the reader that the onlookers "were astounded beyond measure, saying, 'He has done everything well; he even makes the deaf to hear and the mute to speak'" (7:37).

Chapter Four

Jesus the Prophet

A Study of Mark 8:1–10:52

The Third Phase of Jesus' Public Ministry: Second Cycle (8:1–26)

The account of Jesus feeding four thousand persons in Mark 8:1–9 is highly reminiscent of the feeding of the five thousand in Mark 6:30–44. Other elements in 8:1–26 also have parallels with what precedes in 6:30–7:37. Those similarities can be diagrammed as follows:

First Cycle (6:30–7:37)	Second Cycle (8:1–26)
Feeding of 5,000 (6:30–44)	Feeding of 4,000 (8:1–9)
Lake Crossing (6:45–52)	Lake Crossing (8:10)
Controversy with Pharisees (7:1–23)	Controversy with Pharisees (8:11–13)
Children's "Bread" (7:24–30)	Pharisees' "Leaven" (8:14–21)
Deaf-Mute Healed (7:31–37)	Blind Man Healed (8:22–26)

Mark 6:30–8:26, therefore, is composed of two cycles of corresponding incidents. The correlation between the healing of the blind man (8:22–26) and the healing of the deaf-mute (7:31–37) may not be obvious at first. Nevertheless, both healings are performed in private (7:33a; 8:23a), both involve Jesus' use of spittle (7:33b; 8:23b) and the laying on of hands (7:32b, 33b; 8:22b, 23b, 25a), both of the healed persons are charged to secrecy (7:36; 8:26), and both incidents represent "double healings." The former involves the healing of *two ailments,* while the latter involves *two attempts* at healing.

Even though there are clear parallels between the healing of the blind man at Bethsaida (8:22–26) and the healing of the deaf-mute (7:31–37), the uniqueness of the healing of the blind man is difficult to overestimate. For example, this is one Markan healing that is not recorded in either Matthew or Luke. The omission of this account in those later Gospels may be due to the fact that Jesus' first attempt is only partially successful (8:24). Perhaps the later Evangelists did not think that this initial failure was consistent with their respective portraits of Jesus.

The inclusion of this double healing in Mark's Gospel is striking, because up to this point Jesus has been portrayed as a powerful wonder worker. He has already performed flawlessly and effortlessly ten healings and four nature miracles. Jesus has healed several individuals with physical handicaps: a paralytic (2:1–12), a man with a withered hand (3:1–6), and a deaf-mute (7:31–37). Furthermore, Jesus has demonstrated his power over spiritual forces in the various exorcisms that he has performed: a man with an unclean spirit (1:21–28), others who are possessed by demons and unclean spirits (1:34, 39; 3:11–12), the Gerasene demoniac (5:1–20), and the daughter of a Syrophoenician woman (7:24–30). He has demonstrated his power over nature in several nature miracles: stilling the storm (4:35–41), feeding five thousand (6:30–44), walking on water (6:47–52), and feeding four thousand (8:1–9). Therefore, even in the context of Mark's Gospel the double healing of the blind man is contrary to what the reader has come to expect of Jesus.

But the double healing of the blind man is showcased in Mark's Gospel as the *final* miracle of the first half of Mark and the *first* miraculous healing of a blind person. Surely, something motivated Mark to place this miracle story in this climactic position in the Gospel. The double healing of the blind man, which may seem unusual in the context of Mark, actually fits in well with Mark's emphasis on pairs or doublets in the first half of the Gospel. After all, Mark narrates two phases of Jesus' ministry (1:14–3:35 and 4:35–6:6a), both of which are punctuated by visits to his home, then follows that up with two parallel cycles of events (6:30–7:37 and 8:1–26), the second of which concludes with the double healing of the blind man. Perhaps, then, the double healing of the blind man has a more symbolic meaning in its present context. Perhaps this incident reveals that once is not enough. Not everyone who has been "touched" once by Jesus sees clearly. As the blind man's healing suggests, a second touch is needed to bring clear vision. This incident, then, is closely related to what precedes. But as we shall see, the double healing is also related to the confession of Peter that follows (8:27–30).

The Conclusion of the First Half of Mark's Gospel (8:27–30)

Jesus' interrogation of his disciples on their way to Caesarea Philippi (8:27–30) serves as a summary of the first half of the Gospel. In this passage Jesus asks his disciples to tell him, in light of all that he has said and done in the preceding eight chapters, "'Who do people say that I am?'" (8:27). The disciples' answer—"'John the Baptist; and others, Elijah; and still others, one of the prophets'" (8:28)—echoes the earlier editorial remark in Mark, when Herod Antipas was trying to figure out Jesus' identity (6:14–15). These identifications, which attempt to explain Jesus' powerful word and deed as presented in the first half of the Gospel of Mark, also reveal that no one outside Jesus' inner circle truly understands who Jesus is.

When Jesus asks his disciples, "'But who do you say that I am?'" Peter responds, "'You are the Messiah'" (8:29). The Greek word in Peter's confession is *christos*, which the NRSV renders as "Messiah." Although "Messiah" is the Hebrew equivalent of "Christ," the NRSV's use of "Messiah" in 8:29 severs the all-important connection between this critical verse and the first verse of the Gospel. Peter's confession in 8:29 that Jesus is "'the Christ'" is the first occurrence of the key term "Christ" since Mark 1:1.

This, then, represents a significant turning point in the story, because Peter's response signals an apparent change in the disciples. They have been privy to Jesus' secret teaching (4:11–12, 34; 7:17–23) and have witnessed most of his most miraculous deeds, but they have lacked understanding up to this point. After Jesus stills the storm, the disciples ask, "'Who then is this?'" (4:41). After Jesus walks on water, Mark reports that the disciples "did not understand about the [multiplication of the] loaves, but their hearts were hardened" (6:52). After feeding the four thousand, Jesus rebukes his disciples, saying, "'Do you still not perceive or understand? Are your hearts [still] hardened?'" (8:17). With Peter's confession it appears that the disciples have begun to catch on. We know that Peter's confession is accurate, because Jesus "sternly order[s] them not to tell anyone about him" (8:30). This passage continues the messianic secret motif, but Mark 8:30 represents the first time that Jesus commands all of his disciples to secrecy.

With Peter's confession the first half of the Gospel, which portrays Jesus as the powerful Christ, concludes. Although Jesus' miraculous deeds and powerful words have made him popular, they have not revealed his true identity to the multitudes that follow him. The disciples of Jesus, however, now understand who Jesus is. Or do they? The answer to that question lies in what follows.

Jesus' First Passion Prediction and What Follows (8:31–9:29)

The second half of Mark's Gospel (8:31–15:47) portrays Jesus differently than the first half does. It is dominated by the final week of Jesus' life, which leads up to and includes the death of Jesus in Jerusalem. But before Jesus even gets to Jerusalem in 11:1 Mark prepares the reader for what is to come (8:31–10:52). The second half of Mark's Gospel begins, therefore, in Mark 8:31 when Jesus predicts his own death. The reader's attention now turns to the end of the Gospel, for Jesus "began to teach them that the Son of Man must undergo great suffering, and be rejected by the elders, the chief priests, and the scribes, and be killed, and after three days rise again" (8:31). This passage, which previews what lies ahead for Jesus in Jerusalem, is the first explicit reference to Jesus' suffering and death. Jesus' suffering was foreshadowed in the plot of the Pharisees and the Herodians to destroy Jesus (3:6) and in the report of the death of John the Baptist, the forerunner (6:17–29). But in Mark 8:31 Jesus declares exactly what is to happen to him. Since the death of Jesus and the events that immediately precede it are called "the passion," Mark 8:31 is the first *passion prediction* in the Gospel.

When Jesus speaks "quite openly" about his impending death, Peter rebukes him (8:32). On the surface it may look like Peter's rebuke of Jesus is merely an expression of concern for the well-being of a close friend. But Jesus' sharp rebuke of Peter with the words "'Get behind me, Satan! For you are setting your mind not on divine things but on human things'" (8:33) reveals that there is more to this dispute than meets the eye. Actually, the dispute between Peter and Jesus is based on their conflicting views of messiahship.

The first-century Jewish notion of messiah is grounded in the Davidic covenant of 2 Samuel 7. Although God rejects David's kind offer to build God a "house" (= temple; 2 Sam. 7:5), God pledges to build a "house"(= dynasty) for David (2 Sam. 7:11). Then God promises David that his throne "shall be established forever" (2 Sam. 7:16). That promise was made in the tenth century BC.

But in the early sixth century BC—in 587 BC, to be exact—King Zedekiah of Judah rebelled against Babylon (2 Kgs. 24:20b). In response, King Nebuchadnezzar of Babylon and his army laid siege to Jerusalem (2 Kgs. 25:1–3). Although Zedekiah tried to escape from the invading army, Nebuchadnezzar's forces captured Zedekiah and brought him and all of his children before King Nebuchadnezzar (2 Kgs. 25:4–6). After a brief trial, the author reports that, "they slaughtered the sons of Zedekiah before [Zedekiah's] eyes, then put out the eyes of Zedekiah; they bound him in fetters and took him to Babylon" (2 Kgs. 25:7), where he died in exile. In effect, this event brought an end to the Davidic dynasty.

In light of the fall of Jerusalem and the destruction of the Davidic dynasty in 587 BC, God's promise to establish David's throne "forever" had to be reinterpreted. It came to be understood in subsequent centuries that the Davidic covenant must not have been the promise of an unbroken succession of Davidic kings. Rather, by the time of Jesus, Jews understood the promise of 2 Samuel 7 to mean that in the latter days God would raise up *one* king who would rule "forever." Because this king, God's "anointed one" or "messiah," would reign until the end of the age, he would not be subject to death. In first-century Jewish thought, therefore, dying disqualified one from being the Messiah. Gamaliel's speech in Acts 5:36–37 speaks of messianic pretenders who claimed "to be somebody" but turned out not to be when they died. Therefore, when Jesus speaks of his death just after Peter has confessed him as the Messiah, Peter "corrects" Jesus (8:32).

Jesus' rebuke of Peter shows that even though the disciples understand rightly that Jesus is the Christ, they still misunderstand the nature of his messiahship. They cannot grasp the idea that the Messiah must suffer and die. Perhaps this explains why the double healing of the blind man (8:22–26) precedes Peter's confession (8:29). With Peter's confession Peter and the other disciples are beginning to see who Jesus truly is. But the disciples are like the blind man after Jesus touches him for the first time: they can see, but their vision is still clouded. Like the blind man, Peter and the disciples require a "second touch" before they can perceive everything clearly.

After Jesus rebukes Peter (8:33), Jesus begins to teach about discipleship. True disciples will "'deny themselves and take up their cross and follow me'" (8:34b). Only those who "'lose their life for my sake, and for the sake of the gospel, will save it'" (8:35b). In these verses the author has established an important editorial pattern that consists of a passion prediction (8:31), followed by an incident showing the disciples' misunderstanding of what Jesus predicts (8:32–33), followed by a teaching on discipleship (8:34–9:1). The juxtaposition of Jesus' teaching on discipleship with the previous treatment of Jesus' identity and destiny (8:27–31) reveals the close connection between who Christ is and what it means to be a disciple. One must know who Jesus is and where he is going, because Jesus commands his disciples, "'Follow me!'" (8:34b). When Jesus redefines messiahship to include suffering, he also redefines discipleship to include suffering. To follow Jesus is to follow him into suffering (see 10:29–30).

Mark's emphasis on suffering as an essential element of discipleship may have been prompted by the needs of the community that Mark was addressing. That community was a Gentile Christian community, for one would not have had to explain Jewish ritual practices to Jewish Christians (see 7:3–4). The emphasis on suffering and persecution in Mark suggests that this Gentile Christian audience may have been suffering or were facing suffering for their faith. Mark explains that suffering may be a reality at the present time, but suffering will not continue forever. The Son of Man will come "'in the glory of his Father with the holy angels'" at an unspecified time in the future (8:38). Not everyone will "'taste death'" before the kingdom of God comes "'with power'" (9:1).

The story of the transfiguration of Jesus, which occurs "six days later" and takes place on "a high mountain" (9:2), comes next in the narration. This surreal experience begins when Jesus' "clothes became dazzling white, such as no one on earth could bleach them" (9:3), intensifies when Moses and Elijah appear and speak with Jesus (9:4), and climaxes with the voice of God saying, "'This is my Son, the Beloved; listen to him!'" (9:7b). This incident reveals that the Law, represented by the lawgiver Moses, and the Prophets, represented by the prophet Elijah, testify to Jesus. But here the voice of God testifies to Jesus as well. Although God's remarks at the transfiguration are reminiscent of what God said at Jesus' baptism (1:11), the audience has now changed. "'This is my Son, the Beloved,'" as well as the command to "'listen to him,'" are spoken to the disciples. Listen to Jesus about what? In light of the placement of the transfiguration account, God must be referring to Jesus' passion prediction (8:31) and his teaching on discipleship (8:34–9:1). The transfiguration account, therefore, lends additional authoritative support to what Jesus has predicted and taught.

Surely Peter, James, and John, who were with Jesus at the time of his transfiguration, would now know who Jesus truly is. Or would they? As the four are descending the mountain Jesus orders the disciples to keep silent about what they had witnessed "until after the Son of Man ha[s] risen from the dead" (9:9). But Peter, James, and John question "what this rising from the dead could mean" (9:10). Their question about the coming of Elijah (9:11) prompts Jesus to remark that "'the Son of Man . . . is to go through many sufferings and be treated with contempt'" (9:12b). In this brief transitional passage, we have another reference to the impending death and resurrection of Jesus, which is reinforced by Jesus' remark concerning the forerunner John the Baptist, namely, that "'Elijah has come, and they did to him whatever they pleased'" (9:13). But also in these verses we have evidence that the disciples are still not fully aware of who Jesus is and what is in store for him. The following story about the inability of the other disciples at the base of the mountain to heal the demon-possessed boy (9:14–29) underscores the lack of faith on the part of these disciples as well.

Jesus' Second and Third Passion Predictions (9:30–10:52)

As they travel through Galilee, Jesus speaks again to his disciples about his impending death and resurrection: "'The Son of Man is to be betrayed into human hands, and they will kill him, and three days after being killed, he will rise again'" (9:31). This second passion prediction also falls on deaf ears, because the disciples "did not understand what he was saying and were afraid to ask him" (9:32). The disciples' misunderstanding of Jesus and his words is shown by their dispute regarding which of them is the greatest (9:33–34). While Jesus is talking about how he must suffer and die in the near future, the disciples have been arguing about which of them is the best disciple. When Jesus learns of this discussion, he takes this opportunity to speak about discipleship a second time. In order to be first, Jesus explains, one must "'be last of all and servant of all'" (9:35).

Jesus leaves Galilee and travels southward to Judea (10:1). His eventual destination will be Jerusalem, where he will celebrate the Passover, one of three pilgrim feasts in the Jewish ceremonial calendar. As they near Jerusalem, Jesus takes "the twelve aside again" (10:32) in order to tell them what is going to happen to him soon. The third passion prediction, in Mark 10:33–34, is the longest and the most explicit prediction: "'See, we are going up to Jerusalem, and the Son of Man will be handed over to the chief priests and the scribes, and they will condemn him to death; then they will hand him over to the Gentiles; they will mock him, and spit upon him, and flog him, and kill him; and after three days he will rise again.'"

Here, then, is the exact outline of what will happen to Jesus when he arrives in Jerusalem. Jesus could not be any more specific. But the subsequent request of James and John (10:35–37) shows that the disciples still misunderstand the nature of Jesus' messiahship. Thinking that Jesus will be crowned king when he enters Jerusalem, James and John ask Jesus to make them his chief lieutenants (10:37). Jesus' incredulity at their ignorance is expressed in his remark "'You do not know what you are asking'" (10:38a). The request of James and John, the disciples' third instance of misunderstanding, provides a third opportunity for Jesus to teach about discipleship. The greatest disciple is the one who is "'your servant'" and "'slave of all'" (10:43b, 44b), says Jesus, who concludes his teaching on discipleship with the statement that explains his mission and the significance of his death: "'the Son of Man came not to be served but to serve, and to give his life a ransom for many'" (10:45).

This portion of Mark ends with the healing of a blind man named Bartimaeus (10:46–52) who Jesus encounters as he passes through Jericho on his way up to Jerusalem. Blind though he is, Bartimaeus recognizes Jesus as the "'Son of David'" (10:47b, 48b). Jesus responds to Bartimaeus's plea by healing him, and immediately after regaining his sight he follows Jesus (10:51–52).

It is not coincidental that the last healing Jesus performs in Mark's Gospel is the healing of a blind man. Unlike the healing in Mark 8:22–26, however, this time Jesus heals the blind man on the first try. Moreover, it is noteworthy that the two healings of blind persons frame the section containing Jesus' three passion predictions (8:31; 9:31; 10:33–34). Between these two healings of blind people the identity of Jesus is revealed, and what will happen to Jesus in Jerusalem is described in explicit detail. But this section also describes how those closest to Jesus still misunderstand who he is and where he is going. Blind Bartimaeus "sees" who Jesus is more clearly than the sighted characters in the story. The blind man exhibits a faith in Jesus that is sorely lacking in most others. So when he regains his sight, Bartimaeus follows Jesus. But the implication of that observation is that those who do not "see" Jesus clearly will not be able to follow him all the way to the cross.

Chapter Five

The End of Jesus' Public Ministry

A Study of Mark 11:1–14:72

The second half of Mark's Gospel deals with the last part of Jesus' life. Mark's treatment becomes more detailed as Jesus' life comes to an end. In fact, fully one-third of the Gospel (chaps. 11–15) is devoted to the final week of Jesus' life, which takes place in and around Jerusalem. But even before Jesus enters Jerusalem, the reader knows what is in store for him there. On three occasions (8:31; 9:31; 10:33–34) Jesus foretells his suffering, death, and resurrection, so what happens to Jesus in Jerusalem comes as no surprise to the careful reader.

The Beginning of Jesus' Final Week (11:1–26)

The final week begins on a high note, with Jesus' so-called triumphal entry into Jerusalem (11:7–11). That event is preceded by the account of how Jesus secures the animal on which he rides into Jerusalem (11:1–6). To two disciples Jesus gives detailed instructions about where to find "'a colt that has never been ridden'" (11:2b). He even provides them with the words to say when they are challenged by bystanders (11:3b). The fact that the disciples find things just the way Jesus predicted (11:4–6) reveals the keenness of Jesus' prophetic powers as he enters Jerusalem. What Jesus predicts in these chapters will come to pass.

Although Mark does not cite the passage explicitly, Mark's account of Jesus' entry into Jerusalem is informed by Zechariah 9:9: "Rejoice greatly, O daughter Zion! Shout aloud, O daughter Jerusalem! Lo, your king comes to you; triumphant and victorious is he, humble and riding on a donkey, on a colt, the foal of a donkey." Jesus is well received when he enters the city: "Many people spread their cloaks on the road, and others spread leafy branches that they had cut in the fields" (Mark 11:8), while those who accompanied Jesus on that day shouted, "'Hosanna! Blessed is the one who comes in the name of the Lord! Blessed is the coming kingdom of our ancestor David! Hosanna in the highest heaven!'" (11:9b–10). Jesus' companions were probably expecting Jesus to be crowned king on that day. Upon entering Jerusalem, however, Jesus goes to the temple, looks around, and goes back with his disciples to Bethany, where he is staying just a short distance east of Jerusalem (11:11).

On the way into Jerusalem the next day, Jesus performs his final miracle in Mark's Gospel. When he fails to find fruit on a fig tree that he passes along the way, Jesus curses the tree (11:12–14). Cursing miracles are a part of the biblical tradition (see 2 Kgs. 2:23–25), but this is the first and only cursing miracle attributed to Jesus in Mark. What makes this incident even more curious is the observation that "it was not the season for figs" (11:13). Why would Jesus curse a fig tree out of season, and why would Mark include such an odd incident? As was true with the double healing of the blind man (8:22–26), unusual texts in Mark's Gospel are often explained by their juxtaposition to other texts.

When Jesus arrives in Jerusalem, he enters the temple complex for a second time (11:15). The temple was teeming with activity around the time of the Passover. But Jesus brings to a grinding halt the hustle and bustle in the temple: "And he entered the temple and began to drive out those who were selling and those who were buying in the temple, and he overturned the tables of the money changers and the seats of those who sold doves; and he would not allow anyone to carry anything through the temple" (11:15–16).

Jesus goes on to teach the bystanders by citing two passages of Scripture. "'My house shall be called a house of prayer for all the nations'" (11:17a) comes from Isaiah 56:7. Here Jesus charges that the temple is not living up to its intended purpose. The temple is neither "a house of prayer" nor is it "for all nations." The word translated "nations" in this verse is the same term rendered "Gentiles" elsewhere in the New Testament. But Gentiles were strictly prohibited from entering the inner courts of the temple. In fact, an inscription from Herod's temple discovered by archaeologists reads, "No man of another nation [i.e., a Gentile] to enter within the fence and enclosure round the temple. And whoever is caught will have himself to blame that his death ensues."[1]

The second passage Jesus quotes in Mark 11:17b is from the prophet Jeremiah's temple sermon: "'But you have made [the temple] a den of robbers'" (Jer. 7:11). The phrase "den of robbers" in Jeremiah refers not to where robbing takes place but rather to a safe haven where robbers go after they have committed their crimes. Similarly, Jesus charges that the temple has become a safe haven for Israel. The temple gives the Jews a sense of security, for as long as the temple is standing, God's presence is among them, and they can always retreat to the temple to receive God's forgiveness.

When Jesus cleanses the temple he makes some powerful enemies. Those who control the Jerusalem temple are also in the majority on the Sanhedrin, or Council. These Jewish leaders, called "the chief priests and the scribes," are Sadducees. Although the Sadducees were a relatively small sect within first-century Palestinian Judaism, they were very influential. To keep their leadership roles in society they had to work closely with the Romans. To keep Rome at bay, it was to the advantage of the Sadducees to keep things orderly and under control. But when "the chief priests and the scribes" saw what Jesus had done in the temple, "they kept looking for a way to kill him; for they were afraid of him, because the whole crowd was spellbound by his teaching" (11:18). In Mark, as well as in Matthew and Luke, the temple cleansing incident is the beginning of the end for Jesus.

On their way into Jerusalem on the third day the disciples see "the fig tree [that Jesus cursed the day before] withered away to its roots" (11:20). The last miracle that Jesus performs is the only miracle in Mark that does not produce results "immediately." The fig tree withers and dies, but not when Jesus first curses it (11:14). The placement of this story is significant, for the cursing of the fig tree frames the story of Jesus' cleansing of the temple and serves as an interpretive framework for the temple incident. Just as Jesus curses the fig tree for not bearing fruit, so too does Jesus curse the temple for not living up to its intended purpose. Moreover, as Jesus' curse of the fig tree does not result in the immediate destruction of the tree, so too Jesus' curse of the temple does not bring immediate consequences. The temple was destroyed when Jerusalem fell to the Romans in AD 70, some forty years after Jesus' death.

Jesus' subsequent teaching also shows that the temple has outlived its usefulness. No longer does one need to go to the temple to pray and to fulfill the ritual law. Now faith is what is most important, and prayer can be carried out at any time or in any place (11:22–24). Moreover, the sacrifices of the Jerusalem temple are no longer needed for the forgiveness of one's sins. Now, praying to "'your Father in heaven'" and forgiving others is all that is necessary (11:25).

---

1. *The New Testament Background: Selected Documents*, ed. C. K. Barrett (New York: Harper & Row, 1956), 50.

The Conflict with the Religious Authorities Intensifies
(11:27–12:44)

Jesus' third appearance at the Jerusalem temple heightens the animosity that the religious leaders feel toward him. In the temple complex Jesus is challenged by "the chief priests, the scribes, and the elders" about the source of his authority (11:27–28). He refuses to answer their question until they answer his question about the source of John the Baptist's authority (11:29–30). Knowing that they are trapped by the question, they refuse to answer it (11:31–33a). Jesus then refuses to answer their question (11:33b), which does not win Jesus any friends among the Jewish leaders.

Jesus adds insult to injury by telling the parable of the Wicked Tenants. A vineyard owner leaves his vineyard in the hands of tenants who turn out to be untrustworthy (12:1). When the owner sends a series of slaves to receive what belongs to him, the tenants abuse them (12:2–5). Finally, the owner sends "'a beloved son'" (12:6), thinking that the tenants will respect him. But the tenants seize the beloved son, kill him, and cast him out of the vineyard (12:8). In retaliation, says Jesus, the vineyard's owner "'will come and destroy the tenants and give the vineyard to others'" (12:9b).

In this thinly veiled parable Israel is the vineyard and God is the owner. The tenants who have been entrusted to watch over the vineyard are Israel's religious leaders. Those leaders have mistreated God's servants, who are the prophets, and will even abuse God's "'beloved son,'" who is Jesus (see 1:11; 9:7b). Jesus' death, however, has dire consequences for the tenants. The owner of the vineyard "'will come and destroy the tenants and give the vineyard to others'" (12:9b). According to Psalm 118:22–23, which is quoted in Mark 12:10–11, the so-called rejected stone will be vindicated by becoming the cornerstone. All of ""'this was the Lord's doing'"'" (Ps. 118:23; Mark 12:11).

The religious authorities recognize that Jesus "had told this parable against them" (12:12a), which only angers them even more. The irony is that the parable, which predicts the death of Jesus and the involvement of the religious authorities in that death, motivates the religious leaders to seek to destroy Jesus! But the post–AD 70 audience of Mark's Gospel would have recognized that the author is here linking the death of Jesus with the fall of Jerusalem in AD 70, when the Sadducees were wiped out and when Israel was given over to Roman rule exclusively.

The animosity between Jesus and the religious leaders escalates as the religious leaders try to trick Jesus with their questions (12:13–15a, 18–23). But Jesus silences his opponents, who are unable to counter his insightful answers (12:15b–17, 24–27). After Jesus answers accurately a scribe's question concerning the greatest commandment, reports Mark, "no one dared to ask him any question" (12:28–34). Now Jesus asks the religious authorities a question

(12:35–37a), but they cannot answer it. Although "the large crowd was listening to him with delight" (12:37b), the religious authorities are not humored. But Jesus does not stop there. He denounces the influential in society, both the scribes and the rich (12:38–44).

The Synoptic Apocalypse (13:1–37)

Since Mark 8:31, Jesus' power to perform miracles has been on the wane, but his prophetic powers have been on display. Most of what Jesus has prophesied has related to what will happen to him in the near future. He has spoken briefly, however, about the end of time, "'when [the Son of Man] comes in the glory of his Father with the holy angels'" (8:38). Mark 13 is devoted largely to what Jesus teaches will happen before the end.

Although the demise of the temple was implicit in the temple-cleansing incident (11:15–17) and in the cursing of the fig tree (11:12–14, 20–21), Jesus now makes an explicit reference to the temple's future destruction (13:2). When Peter, James, John, and Andrew ask him in private about the end of time, Jesus describes the false prophets that will arise and the other disasters that will occur but cautions that "'this is but the beginning of the birth pangs'" (13:3–8). He enumerates the persecutions that can be anticipated and other signs that are expected, then he warns his disciples, "'Be alert; I have already told you everything'" (13:9–23). Then, "'after that suffering,'" the eschatological or end-time Son of Man will come with unmistakable signs and wonders (13:24–26). He will "'send out the angels, and gather his elect from the four winds, from the ends of the earth to the ends of heaven'" (13:27). Like the fig tree, we can know the season when "'he is near'" (13:29), but "'about that [specific] day or [exact] hour no one knows, neither the angels in heaven, nor the Son, but only the Father'" (13:32). The message of the chapter is "'Beware, keep alert'" (13:33) and "'keep awake'" (13:35, 37), for the end-time is coming (13:30), but no one knows when.

The Climax of Two Markan Themes (14:1–72)

In chapter 14 two prominent Markan themes come to a climax. Prior to Peter's confession in Mark 8:29, the disciples lack understanding about who Jesus is (4:41; 6:51–52; 8:17–18, 21), even though they were privy to Jesus' private instruction (4:11–12, 34) and witnessed some of the most amazing miracles, which others did not see (4:35–41; 5:35–43; 6:45–52; 7:31–37; 8:22–26). After Peter's confession in Mark 8:29 the disciples' lack of understanding turns to misunderstanding about who Jesus is and what he must suffer, as illustrated by

Peter's rebuke (8:32b), the debate concerning who is the greatest (9:33–34), and the request of James and John (10:35–40).

The disciples' misunderstanding takes a tragic turn in Mark 14. This is not unexpected. Jesus' teaching on discipleship (8:34–9:1; 9:35–37; 10:42–45) relates true discipleship to the identity and destiny of Jesus. One must know where Jesus is going if one is going to follow him. The disciples' misunderstanding of Jesus' identity and his destiny foreshadows the disciples' failure to follow Jesus to the end.

That failure begins during the Last Supper when Jesus predicts that a disciple will betray him (14:18, 20). Then on the Mount of Olives Jesus predicts that his disciples will all desert him (14:27) and that Peter will deny him (14:30). These three prophecies are fulfilled by the end of chapter 14. In the garden of Gethsemane, Judas betrays Jesus (14:43–45) and his disciples desert him (14:50). Later that evening, Peter denies him three times (14:66–72). After Peter breaks down and weeps (14:72b), the disciples are completely out of the picture. They are not present at the crucifixion, nor are they there for the burial of Jesus. They are not at the tomb on the first day of the week, so they are not the first ones to know that Jesus has been raised from the dead.

The theme of Jesus' conflict with the religious authorities also reaches its climax in chapter 14. The chapter begins with the chief priests and scribes plotting against Jesus (14:1–2). They are "looking for a way to arrest Jesus by stealth and kill him" (14:1b), so when Judas comes to them "in order to betray [Jesus] to them . . . they [are] greatly pleased" (14:10b–11a).

At an opportune time Judas leads "a crowd . . . from the chief priests, the scribes, and the elders" to arrest Jesus in the garden of Gethsemane (14:43–50). After the arrest, Jesus is taken to the high priest to appear before "the whole council" (14:55). This council, the Sanhedrin, was composed of "the chief priests, the elders, and the scribes" (14:53; see also 15:1), which is exactly the group of Jews that Jesus had already succeeded in alienating (11:18, 27; 12:12). The trial of Jesus (14:55–65) brings to a climax the opposition between Jesus and the religious authorities. One cannot expect a fair trial for Jesus before a group portrayed as totally devoted to his destruction (14:1). The trial begins with the court committed to a guilty verdict (14:55–56a). The only challenge is finding a charge that will stick!

Many testify falsely against Jesus, but none of the testimony can be corroborated (14:56–59). When Jesus refuses to answer any of the false charges, the high priest blurts out, "'Are you the Messiah, the Son of the Blessed One?'" (14:60–61). As in 8:29, the term rendered "Messiah" in the New Revised Standard Version translation of 14:61 is the Greek word *christos*. The term "Christ," as previously noted, is rare in Mark's Gospel, found only in the prologue (1:1), on the lips of Peter (8:29), and in only a few other places (9:41; 12:35; 13:21; 15:32). "Son of God," on the other hand, is a title found in the prologue (1:1), at Jesus' baptism (1:11), at the transfiguration (9:7), and in the rantings of some demons (3:11; 5:7). The high priest's query in Mark 14:61b is the *first* occurrence since Mark 1:1 of the "Christ" title with the "Son of God" designation.

Note that the high priest does not use the word "God" in his question of 14:61b, because the name of God was deemed unpronounceable. The unpronounceable name is God's personal name that God revealed to Moses at the burning bush in Exodus 3. That name consists of four consonants, YHWH, that are thought to come from the Hebrew verb "to be." For that reason, modern translations like the New Revised Standard Version render the personal name that God reveals in Exodus 3:14 as "I AM." In the Greek translation of the Hebrew Bible, the "I AM" of Exodus 3:14 is rendered as *ego eimi*. In order to avoid breaking the commandment that forbids making "wrongful use of the name of the LORD [Heb. *YHWH*] your God" (Exod. 20:7), Jews avoided using the personal name of God altogether, as the high priest did in his question to Jesus. To utter God's personal name was considered blasphemy.

In Mark 14:62 Jesus responds to the high priest's question by saying, "I am" (Gk. *ego eimi*), when a simple *eimi* ("I am") would have sufficed. In acknowledging his true identity, Jesus commits blasphemy by uttering the unspeakable name of God. With Jesus' acknowledgment of his true identity, the messianic secret is exposed. At the moment that Jesus' identity is fully revealed, however, he is condemned to death. The high priest tears his clothes and says, "'You have heard [Jesus'] blasphemy!'" and the council has also heard what Jesus says. As a result, reports Mark, "all of them condemned him as deserving death" (14:64).

The story of Peter's denial (14:54, 66–72) brackets the trial of Jesus (14:53, 55–65), but the denial by Peter outside in the courtyard is to be understood as happening at the same time as the trial of Jesus inside. Peter's "trial," in fact, stands in contrast to Jesus' trial. As Jesus is being examined by the high priest inside (14:53), Peter is being examined by "one of the servant-girls of the high priest" (14:66, 69) outside. When Jesus is confronted by his enemies, he stands firm and acknowledges his true identity (14:62), even though it means his death (14:64). In contrast, Peter collapses under pressure and denies Jesus three times in order to spare his own life (14:68, 70, 71). After the trial, when Jesus is blindfolded, beaten, and told to prophesy on the inside (14:65), the cock is crowing for a second time and Peter is weeping outside, because Jesus' prophecy about Peter's denial (14:30) has been fulfilled (14:72). Moreover, Jesus' trial before the Sanhedrin fulfills Jesus' prediction that he would "be rejected by the elders, the chief priests, and the scribes" (8:31). Jesus' accusers taunt him by saying, "'Prophesy!'" (14:65), when all that happens to Jesus in the second half of Mark 14 fulfills the prophecies that Jesus made earlier in the Gospel.

Chapter Six

The End of the Gospel?

A Study of Mark 15:1–16:8

The Death of Jesus: An Interpretive Note (15:1–15a)

Jesus' being "handed over" to Pilate (15:1) fulfills the third passion prediction that says the chief priests and the scribes "'will condemn him to death; then they will hand him over to the Gentiles'" (10:33–34). In order to appreciate Mark's perspective in chapter 15, the reader needs to be aware of two historical facts.

Fact 1: The Romans killed Jesus. All sources agree that Jesus died by crucifixion (Mark 15:21–39; Matt. 27:32–44; Luke 23:26–43; John 19:16b–27; see also 1 Cor. 1:23; 2:2, 8; 2 Cor. 13:4; Gal. 2:19–20), and crucifixion was a Roman form of punishment. Jews did not crucify wrongdoers. If Jesus had been found guilty of blasphemy, as Mark states (14:64), then the appropriate Jewish form of capital punishment would have been stoning (Lev. 24:13–16), which Stephen received in Acts 7:58–59.

Furthermore, all of the sources agree that Jesus was executed as the "King of the Jews" (Mark 15:26; Matt. 27:37; Luke 23:38; John 19:19). This is the formal charge against Jesus. This charge also supports the notion of Roman execution, for "King of the Jews" is an expression used by non-Jews (Mark 15:2, 9,

12, 18; see Matt. 2:2; 27:11, 29, 37; Luke 23:3, 37–38; John 18:33, 39; 19:3, 14, 19, 21). Jews talk about the Messiah as the "King of Israel" (Mark 15:32; Matt. 27:42; John 1:49; 12:13).

Fact 2: The leaders of the Jews had a hand in Jesus' demise. All of the sources agree, but they disagree on the extent of this participation. Much of Mark 11–14 is concerned with showing the prominent role of the Jewish religious authorities in the events that lead up to Jesus' death. Mark highlights the active participation of one group within that leadership, namely, the chief priests and their scribes, who were Sadducees. Jesus predicts their involvement before he enters Jerusalem (10:33). Later, the chief priests want to arrest and kill Jesus (14:1). When Judas decides to betray Jesus, he goes to the chief priests (14:10), who agree to pay Judas a bounty for his services (14:11b). The chief priests are a part of the council (14:53), so the chief priests in general and the high priest (who is also a Sadducee) in particular play a prominent role in the trial of Jesus before the council (14:53, 55, 60, 61b, 63–64). The chief priests then hand Jesus over to Pilate (15:1b), accuse Jesus of many wrongdoings (15:3), stir up the crowd to have Barabbas released instead of Jesus (15:11), and mock Jesus as he hangs on the cross (15:31–32a).

Mark, therefore, describes a select group of Jews who participated in the plot against Jesus. The size of "the crowd" that the chief priests stir up (15:8, 11, 13, 14b, 15) is unknown, but this was surely a vocal minority of the Jewish population in Jerusalem at the time. In fact, the arrest and trial of Jesus had to have been done under the cover of night, because the chief priests are afraid that there "'may be a riot among the people'" (14:2). The devious methods of the chief priests, therefore, are necessitated by the popularity of Jesus with "the people" in Jerusalem. Only a relatively small but influential group of Jewish leaders in Jerusalem opposed Jesus actively.

By accentuating the involvement of the Jewish leaders in Jerusalem, Mark lessens Roman responsibility, which is evident in Jesus' trial before Pilate (15:1–15a). In Mark's account Pilate does everything he can to have Jesus released. Pilate is "amazed," not angered, at Jesus' unwillingness to answer the charges brought against him (15:5). Pilate recognizes that "it was out of jealously that the chief priests had handed him over" (15:10). Pilate acknowledges Jesus' innocence when he says, "'Why, what evil has he done?'" (15:14). Pilate even tries to free Jesus through his annual program of prisoner release (15:6–7), but the crowd, under the influence of the chief priests, demands the release of the insurrectionist Barabbas instead (15:8, 11). After more shouting Pilate finally surrenders to the crowd's wishes by releasing Barabbas and turning Jesus over to be crucified (15:15).

Twenty-first-century readers must be careful in their understanding of this material, for much anti-Jewish thought has resulted from this account. We must appreciate Mark's perspective but also be critical of it, for Mark's version was historically conditioned. It was politically expedient to have a Roman official declare Jesus' innocence, for this would have proven to Roman leaders that Jesus and his followers were never perceived as a threat to Rome. But Mark emphasizes the suffering of Jesus and stresses suffering as the confirmation of true discipleship, which suggests that Mark was writing for a community that had suffered, was currently suffering, or was about to suffer persecution (see 10:30; 13:9–13). The unusual emphasis on the Jewish rather than the Roman role in the events surrounding Jesus' death may indicate that the source of the early community's persecution was Jewish (see 13:9a). Mark's message is that true followers of Jesus can expect suffering at the hands of the Jews, for that is exactly what happened to the Master.

In reality, however, the Jews were *less* responsible and the Romans were *more* responsible for the death of Jesus than Mark's account would have us believe. Moreover, the Sadducees, that Jewish sect Mark describes as being so involved in the events leading to Jesus' death, did not survive the first century AD. What Jesus predicted in the parable of the Wicked Tenants (12:1–11), that the owner of the vineyard will "'destroy the tenants and give the vineyard to others'" (12:9b), came to pass in the destruction of Jerusalem and the temple by the Romans in AD 70. By the time Mark wrote his Gospel, therefore, the Sadducees were gone. The Pharisees were the only Jewish sect that survived the fall of Jerusalem.

The Crucifixion, Death, and Burial of Jesus (15:15b–47)

Pilate then hands Jesus over to his soldiers for scourging and crucifixion (15:15b–20). Mark's account of Jesus' crucifixion is striking for what it omits, for there is no reference to the unbelievable physical suffering or to the utter degradation and humiliation that crucifixion represented. Mark reports matter-of-factly, "and they crucified him" (15:24a). Surely, first-century readers would not need a detailed description of this cruel form of punishment, because crucifixions were commonplace in the Roman Empire. Without any written description, however, those unfamiliar with this type of capital punishment could only speculate about how crucifixions were carried out.

Crucifixion was not invented by the Romans, but it was perfected by them, for the Romans executed thousands of persons by this cruel and unusual form of punishment. Only males were crucified, and only those who were guilty of the most serious crimes were subjected to this gruesome form of punishment. The purpose of crucifixion was not to kill but to prolong the death of the criminal to the point where he would beg to be killed.

Crucifixion began with flogging or scourging (see 15:15b). Criminals who were condemned to death were stripped, and their hands were tied to a post.

They were then beaten with a whip composed of leather straps that were bound together into a handle. Each strip had on the other end a leather ball in which were embedded pieces of metal or bone to aggravate the torture. This whip would quickly shred the flesh of a prisoner's naked back, arms, shoulders, legs, and buttocks. The result of this torture (which was sometimes fatal) was significant loss of blood through many open wounds. With the loss of blood, the prisoner's blood-sugar level dropped precipitously, so that the prisoner was less able to resist the rest of the punishment.

After the scourging, prisoners were then forced to walk to the place of execution by a circuitous route. Most prisoners carried the instrument of their own death, the cross. This lengthy and very public parade was meant to exhaust the prisoner and deter any onlooker from attempting a similar crime. Criminals usually carried only the crossbar, to which their arms were often tied. The upright piece of the cross was already permanently embedded at the site of execution. That someone else was "compelled. . .to carry [Jesus'] cross" (15:21) reveals how badly Jesus was beaten during his flogging.

Although crucifixion was practiced widely in the Roman Empire, we did not know exactly how persons were crucified in Palestine in the first century until the 1960s, when the skeletal remains of a man who was killed by crucifixion were unearthed in a first-century tomb in Jerusalem. It was widely thought that only Jesus had been nailed to the cross, perhaps as a special form of punishment. The skeletal remains of the man crucified in Jerusalem, however, show marks of nailing, and a bent nail remains in some bones.

In light of these skeletal remains, it appears that the arms of prisoners were pinned to the cross by a nail driven between the two bones of the forearm (the radius and the ulna) above the wrist. This makes sense, because a nail simply driven through the palm would not have been able to support the weight of a person hanging on the cross. Besides, the term "hand" in antiquity referred to the entire end of one's arm and not simply to the palm and fingers, so the references to Jesus having nail prints in his "hands" in Luke 24:39–40 and in John 20:20, 25, 27 can be reconciled with the archaeological evidence.

Once the arms were nailed to the crossbar, the victim was lifted up and the crossbar was secured to the upright that was embedded in the ground. The legs were then fastened to the upright with a single nail driven through the heel bones. The bent nail that remains in the heel bones of the first-century man has some acacia wood on it, which indicates that a piece of wood was placed over the site of nailing. The nail penetrated the wood before entering the victim's flesh and bone.

The nailing, which was painful but not lethal, pinned the prisoner in a position that made breathing difficult. In order to breathe, a prisoner had to lift himself up, but to do so he had to push down on his legs, which were nailed to the cross. Lifting himself up also caused his very tender back to scrape along the rough wood of the cross. Add to this the discomfort caused by the heat of the day and the cold of the night, the annoyance of the insects and the birds that flew around his body, and the humiliation of being strung up not far off the ground and stark naked for the world to see.

Death came when the prisoner could no longer lift himself up to get a breath. This could be the result of the great loss of blood and of incredible fatigue. To speed up the process the guards might take a club and break the lower legs of the person being crucified, which in turn prevented him from being able to push up to breathe. Death came from asphyxiation. In some cases, people lasted for several days on the cross. According to Mark's account, Jesus was on the cross a mere six hours, from 9 a.m. (15:25) to 3 p.m. (15:33), another sign of the brutal flogging Jesus must have endured.

Again, Mark's account of Jesus' crucifixion is distinctive because of its notable absences. Mark does not mention the physical, psychological, and emotional torment that such persons felt. Instead, Mark portrays Jesus dying among hostile, unbelieving, uncaring people. Passers-by, chief priests and their scribes, and even those crucified with Jesus (15:29–32) taunt him, while those who had been closest to Jesus are at that moment farthest from him. All of the disciples fled by the end of chapter 14, and only a few women "looked on from a distance" (15:40–41). The overwhelming aloneness of Jesus on the cross stands in sharp contrast to Jesus' overwhelming popularity in the first part of Mark's Gospel (1:28, 33, 45; 3:8–9; 6:34–44; 8:6–9). Jesus even feels abandoned by God, as his chilling cry, "'My God, my God, why have you forsaken me?'" (15:34; Ps. 22:1a) suggests. But Jesus is misunderstood, even on the cross, for some onlookers think that his cry "'Eloi, Eloi'" is addressed to Elijah (15:35–36). Then Jesus simply utters "a loud cry" and dies unceremoniously (15:37).

Two important events occur at the moment of Jesus' death. The temple curtain that separates the innermost sanctum, known as the holy of holies, from the outer temple chamber is torn in two (15:38). Once a year, on the Day of Atonement (Yom Kippur) before AD 70, the high priest would go behind that curtain, enter the holy of holies, and seek forgiveness for the sins of the people of Israel. The rending of this curtain at the moment of Jesus' death may signify that believers now have free access to God's forgiveness. But the destruction of the curtain also seals the fate of the now obsolete temple.

Jesus' death also elicits the centurion's confession, "'Truly this man was God's Son!'" (15:39). It is not insignificant that the first one to recognize Jesus as the Son of God is a Gentile, a Roman centurion, for there are indications that this work was written to a Gentile audience (see 7:3–4), which explains why Gentiles are portrayed in a positive light in the Gospel (see 7:24–30). But it is also worth noting that what prompts the centurion's confession is seeing Jesus die. It is in his death that Jesus' true identity is finally and fully revealed. What Jesus' miraculous works were unable to do, his suffering and death are able to do.

The corpses of those crucified usually were allowed to hang on the cross until they decomposed or were devoured by predatory birds or animals. Whether Joseph of Arimathea, who is described as "a respected member of the council" (15:43a)—which had earlier condemned Jesus (14:55–65; 15:1)—is a closet Jesus-sympathizer or is an enemy-turned-friend of Jesus is not stated in the text. This Joseph asks Pilate for permission to remove Jesus' body from the cross (15:43b) for the purpose of burying Jesus before sundown. Jesus "had been dead for some time" (15:44b), so permission is granted, and the body is removed. Because it is getting late and the onset of the Sabbath is fast approaching, Joseph only has time to wrap Jesus' body in a linen cloth and put it in a nearby tomb before rolling a stone over the entrance (15:46). Some of the female onlookers see where Joseph buries Jesus (15:47), so they know where to come "very early on the first day of the week" (16:2).

The Epilogue: The Empty Tomb (16:1–8)

According to the most ancient extant manuscript evidence, the text of Mark's Gospel ends with 16:8. Mark 16:9–20, which is included in some later Greek manuscripts, forms an ancient appendix that was not an original part of Mark's work. The style and vocabulary of 16:9–20 provide another clue that this is not the work of the author of the rest of the Gospel. But Mark 16:8 is an unusual place to end the Gospel.

After the Sabbath three women go to anoint Jesus' body (16:1–3). Upon arriving at the tomb where Jesus was laid out, the women find the tomb open (16:4). Instead of finding the lifeless body of Jesus inside, the women encounter an angelic being who informs them of Jesus' resurrection and then commands them to "'go, tell his disciples and Peter that he is going ahead of you to Galilee; there you will see him, just as he told you'" (16:5–7). The Gospel ends abruptly with the statement that "they said nothing to anyone, for they were afraid" (16:8). If 16:8 is the last verse of the work, then the Greek text of Mark ends with the preposition "for," and the Gospel concludes before any appearances of the risen Lord occur. It is easy to see why later copyists felt the need to add to the ending of this work.

But the fact remains that the Gospel of Mark ends at 16:8, and it is important to make sense of this ending. First of all, the Gospel does not need resurrection appearances. This Gospel was written for believers (see 1:1) who do not require proof that Jesus was raised from the dead. This audience is already aware of Jesus' resurrection. They are told about the resurrection in Mark 16:6. Besides, Jesus foretold his resurrection on numerous occasions (8:31; 9:9, 31; 10:34) and explained to his disciples on the Mount of Olives, "'After I am raised up, I will go before you to Galilee'" (14:28).

Like other parts of Mark, however, the ending is ironic. In the early chapters of the Gospel, people are repeatedly told to be quiet about what they see and hear. Nevertheless, they "talk freely" (see 1:45; 7:36). Now when the time has finally come to spread the news, the women are afraid and tell no one. How ironic is that!

From the very beginning of Mark the narrative has proceeded on two levels. One level is what the characters in the story know, and the other level is what the readers know. The readers, however, have had a significant advantage over the characters in the story, because the readers know how the story ends. Those who walked with and talked to Jesus during his earthly ministry could not fully comprehend his identity. They had only "partial vision." But all subsequent readers who know about Jesus' death and resurrection have received that "second touch" that the blind man of Mark 8:22–26 required. The readers of Mark begin their encounter with "the gospel" fully aware that Jesus is the "Christ, the Son of God" (1:1).

So apart from the women who visit the tomb, the only ones who know of Christ's resurrection are the readers. Since the women "said nothing to anyone" (16:8), then the good news would die unless the readers testified to what they know. Therefore, at the very end of the work, the Evangelist throws the burden of proclamation into the readers' lap. From the outset the readers have been watching passively as the story unfolds. Now it is time for knowledgeable readers to act. The ending of Mark's Gospel enlists them to do what the women do not do: "'Go, tell'" (16:7).

This interpretation fits well with Mark 1:1, "The beginning of the good news of Jesus Christ, the Son of God." The first verse is, as in much ancient literature, the title of the whole work. But this sixteen-chapter story is only "the beginning." It is by no means the entire story. Present readers must become a part of that story through their proclaiming it (see 13:10) and their consequent suffering in the world (10:30; 13:9–13), all the while confident and ever watchful for the return of the Son of Man """"with the clouds of heaven"""" (14:62; also 8:38b; 13:26–27).

Outline of the Gospel of Mark

I. The Prologue: Before Jesus' Public Ministry (1:1–13)

    A. Superscription (1:1)

    B. John as Forerunner (1:2–8, 14a)

    C. Jesus Is Baptized by John (1:9–11)

    D. Jesus Is Tempted in the Wilderness (1:12–13)

II. "The Powerful Christ" (1:14–8:30)

    A. The First Phase of Jesus' Public Ministry (1:14–3:35)

        1. Jesus' First Preaching (1:14–15)

        2. Jesus Calls Simon and Andrew, James and John (1:16–20)

        3. Miracle 1: Exorcism in the Synagogue in Capernaum (1:21–28)

        4. Miracle 2: Curing the Fever of Simon's Mother-in-Law (1:29–31)

        5. Jesus Heals Others (1:32–34)

        6. Galilean Preaching Tour (1:35–39)

        7. Miracle 3: Cleansing a Leper (1:40–45)

        8. Miracle 4: Healing a Paralytic (2:1–12)

        9. Controversy with the Pharisees over Eating Regulations (2:13–22)

            a. Jesus Calls Levi (2:13–14)

            b. Jesus Criticized for Eating with Tax Collectors and Sinners (2:15–17)

            c. Jesus Criticized because His Disciples Do Not Fast (2:18–22)

        10. More Controversy with the Pharisees over Sabbath Observance (2:23–3:6)

            a. Jesus Criticized When the Disciples "Work" on the Sabbath (2:23–28)

            b. Miracle 5: Healing a Man's Withered Hand on the Sabbath (3:1–6)

        11. Jesus' Popularity Spreads (3:7–12)

        12. Jesus Appoints Twelve Apostles (3:13–19a)

        13. Jesus Returns Home (3:19b–35)

            a. Reaction of Jesus' Family (3:21)

            b. Reaction of the Scribes from Jerusalem (3:22, 30)

            c. Jesus Rebuts the Scribes from Jerusalem (3:23–29)

            d. Jesus' True Family (3:31–35)

    B. Interlude: Jesus Teaches in Parables (4:1–34)

    C. The Second Phase of Jesus' Public Ministry (4:35–6:6a)

        1. (Super)Miracle 6: Stilling the Storm (4:35–41)

        2. (Super)Miracle 7: Healing the Gerasene Demoniac (5:1–20)

Outline of the Gospel of Mark *(continued)*

      3. (Super)Miracle 8: Healing a Hemorrhaging Woman (5:24b–34)

      4. (Super)Miracle 9: Raising Jairus's Daughter from the Dead (5:21–24a, 35–43)

      5. Jesus Returns Home Again and Is Rejected (6:1–6a)

    D. Interlude (6:6b–29)

      1. Jesus Commissions the Twelve (6:7–13)

      2. The Death of John the Baptist Narrated (6:14–29)

    E. The Third Phase of Jesus' Public Ministry (6:30–8:26)

      1. First Cycle (6:30–7:37)

        a. Miracle 10: Feeding of the Five Thousand (6:30–44)

        b. Miracle 11: Lake Crossing, with Jesus Walking on Water (6:45–52)

        c. Jesus' Popularity as a Wonder Worker Described (6:53–56)

        d. Controversy with the Pharisees over the Oral Law (7:1–23)

        e. Miracle 12: Exorcism of the Syrophoenician Woman's Daughter after a Discussion about Bread (7:24–30)

        f. Miracle 13: Healing of the Deaf Mute (7:31–37)

      2. Second Cycle (8:1–26)

        a. Miracle 14: Feeding of the Four Thousand (8:1–9)

        b. Lake Crossing (8:10)

        c. Controversy with Pharisees Who Demand a Sign from Jesus (8:11–13)

        d. Discussion with Disciples concerning Bread (8:14–21)

        e. Miracle 15: Double Healing of Blind Man (8:22–26)

    F. The Conclusion of the First Half of Mark's Gospel: Peter's Confession (8:27–30)

III. "The Suffering Christ" (8:31–15:47)

    A. Before Entering Jerusalem (8:31–10:52)

      1. First Cycle (8:31–9:29)

        a. Jesus' First Passion Prediction (8:31)

        b. Disciples' First Misunderstanding: Peter's Rebuke (8:32–33)

        c. Jesus Teaches on Discipleship (8:34–9:1)

        d. The Transfiguration and Afterward (9:2–13)

        e. Miracle 16: Exorcism of the Boy with an Unclean Spirit (9:14–29)

      2. Second Cycle (9:30–10:31)

        a. Jesus' Second Passion Prediction (9:31)

        b. Disciples' Second Misunderstanding: Greatest Disciple (9:32–34)

        c. Jesus Teaches on Discipleship a Second Time (9:35–37)

Outline of the Gospel of Mark *(continued)*

Outline of the Gospel of Mark *(continued)*

Part Two

LEADER'S GUIDE

DONALD L. GRIGGS

Guidelines for Bible Study Leaders

Goals of the Course

Even though a reader could study this course on the Gospel of Mark without being a member of a class, the greatest value will be realized when the reader is engaged with others who are companions on the journey. As I have prepared these session plans I have had in mind several goals that I hope participants will experience as a result of their study. I hope that the participants will

- bring to their study a desire to enter more deeply into the world of the Bible, specifically in this study, the world of the Gospel of Mark;

- enjoy studying the Bible with others;

- come to a greater understanding and appreciation of the structure and message of the Gospel of Mark;

- bring their insights, questions, and affirmations prompted through their study to share with others; and

- develop a discipline of reading and studying the Bible on a regular basis.

Basic Teaching Principles

In these session plans I have worked hard to implement a number of basic principles for effective teaching and leading. The foundational principle is an attempt to involve everyone in the class in as many activities as possible for every session. That's a big goal, but there are many opportunities for individuals to participate every week, and most will if they are encouraged to do so. You will see this principle present in all of the session plans that follow. Here are the other principles I had in mind as I designed this course:

- The leader serves best as companion and guide in the journey of the course.

- The leader provides sufficient information, but not so much that the joy of discovery by the participants is lost.

- Motivation for learning involves enjoying and completing tasks, and making choices.

- Participants learn best when a variety of activities and resources are used in order to respond to their different interests, needs, and learning styles.

- Participants need to be invited to express their feelings, ideas, and beliefs in ways that are appropriate to them and to the subject matter.

- Everyone needs opportunities to share what they understand and believe.

- Open-ended questions invite interpretation, reflection, and application.

- Persons are nurtured in faith when they share their faith stories with one another.

- All teaching and learning happens in planned and unplanned ways and is for the purpose of increasing biblical literacy and faithful discipleship.

- The Bible becomes the living word of God when teachers and learners see Scripture connecting to their own faith stories.

- The Bible provides many resources to prompt our praying, our confessing of faith, and our committing ourselves to the ministry of Jesus Christ.

Room Arrangement

Arrange the room where you meet in such a way that participants are seated at tables. Tables are very important in that they provide space for all of the materials and the coffee cups. They also suggest that we are going to work; we are not to just sit and listen to a lecture. If the class members do not all know each other, then they all need name tags. Set up a table with hot water and makings for coffee, tea, and hot chocolate just inside the entrance to the room so everyone can get a cup and then find a seat. If you have a small group, arrange the tables in a rectangle or square so that everyone can see all the other members of the group. With a small group you will be able to be seated with them. On the other hand, if you have a large group, arrange the tables in a fan shape pointed toward the front so the participants can see you standing at the front of the group with a whiteboard, newsprint easel, or bulletin board.

Resources

For the first session, provide Bibles for those who did not bring one. Continue to provide Bibles for those occasions when it is important for everyone to have the same translation and edition if you plan for them all to look at the same pages at the same time. However, encourage participants to bring their own Bibles. In addition to the Bibles, borrow copies of concise concordances, Bible dictionaries, commentaries on Mark, and Bible atlases from the church library, the pastor's library, and your own library. A church library will not ordinarily have enough Bible dictionaries for each person to have one, so for those sessions where members will be asked to search for information about a passage, person, or event in Mark, make photocopies of the appropriate articles in a Bible dictionary, encyclopedia, or atlas. For one-time use, for one class, this is not a violation of the copyright laws.

Provide paper and pencils for those who don't bring them. Almost all of the activity sheets to be used by the participants are at the end of the session plans for which they will be used.

Time

I planned each session to be an hour in length. If you have less than an hour, you will have to make some adjustments. It will be better to leave an activity out than to rush class members through all of the planned activities. Perhaps it would be possible in your situation to schedule more than six sessions. There is probably enough material here for eight to ten sessions. If you had that much time you would truly be able to deal with everything carefully, without hurrying.

If you and your group have not already studied the first two books in this Bible study series, *The Bible from Scratch: The Old Testament for Beginners* and *The Bible from Scratch: The New Testament for Beginners*, you may find it helpful to use session 1 from either of those courses as an introduction to this style of Bible study.

Final Word

As you prepare to teach this course, it is essential that you read each chapter of the Participant's Guide as you consider your teaching strategy for each session. You should assume that many of the participants will have read the respective chapter before coming to the class session, and you should be as familiar with the material as they are. Exploring the Gospel of Mark with fellow pilgrims on the journey of faith will be for them and for you a challenging, inspiring, growing, and satisfying experience. May God bless you with many discoveries and much joy on this journey. If you and the members of your Bible study group have found this course to be helpful, you may want to plan for other "From Scratch" Bible studies that will appear in the series.

Session One

The Genius of Mark
the Evangelist

An Introduction to the Study of Mark's Gospel

BEFORE THE SESSION
Focus of the Session

This session will focus on some of the characteristics of the Gospel of Mark that distinguish it from the other three Gospels, especially Matthew and Luke. The matters of the Synoptic Problem and the Gospel of Mark as the first Gospel will be explored. This session will provide an introduction into the structure and unique message of Mark.

Advance Preparation

- Take the time to read the whole of the Gospel of Mark. Try to do it in one sitting.

- Read an introductory article or two about Mark in a study Bible and/or Bible dictionary.

- Read articles in a Bible dictionary that deal with "Gospel" and "synoptic."

- Gather several Bible study tools to share with the participants: a single-volume Bible commentary and a commentary on the Gospel of Mark, a Gospel parallels book, a Bible dictionary, and one or more study Bibles.

- Duplicate the worksheet "'Immediately' in the First Half of Mark's Gospel."

- Provide a few extra Bibles for those who forget to bring one.

Physical Arrangements

Reread the section in "Guidelines for Bible Study Leaders" that offers suggestions regarding room arrangement, resources and materials, and refreshments. You should have everything ready for the first session. You will want to make a good first impression, especially for those who are new to Bible study.

Teaching Alternatives

The session plan that follows assumes a minimum of one hour for the study. If you have less than an hour, you will need to make some adjustments in the plan. You could consider several possibilities: (1) extend the session to two sessions, (2) skip the "Building Community" activity if the members of the group already know each other fairly well, or (3) eliminate the "Exploring 'Immediately'" activity.

DURING THE SESSION
Welcoming the Participants

Arrive early enough to set up the refreshments and to have everything ready before the first persons arrive. Ask the participants to sign in and make name tags for themselves. Greet each one by name and with a warm welcome. Check to see who needs to borrow a Bible, and give them one. Encourage everyone to bring a Bible to the next session. If any of the participants do not already have a copy of this course book, give them one so they will have access to the references you make to it during the session.

Introducing the Course

After all have arrived and you have welcomed them, share with the group an overview of what to expect in this course. Emphasize these points:

- This first session will be an introduction to the Gospel of Mark.

- The remaining five or more sessions will move sequentially through the Gospel.

- The session plans will not necessarily repeat what is in part 1 but will be based upon that material and the related portions of Mark.

- It is expected that participants will read the relevant chapter in the Participant's Guide in preparation for each session.

- Everyone should bring a Bible to class, preferably a study Bible. Spend a few minutes showing the value of a study Bible. Recommended study Bibles are described on page 115 in the appendix.

- Suggest that everyone's understanding and appreciation of Mark will be enhanced greatly if they are able to read the sixteen chapters of the Gospel in one sitting. They can do it in less than two hours.

- There will be some presentation by the leader in each session, but most of the time the leader will be guiding the class members through a series of activities designed to engage them with the key Scriptures and main ideas of that session.

- There are no "dumb questions." All questions are appropriate. Encourage the participants to ask questions of the leader and the group.

- Everyone's insights, ideas, and affirmations will be received and respected. It is important to feel free to express what is on one's mind and heart.

- This journey through the Gospel of Mark will begin with a brief litany prayer.

Opening Prayer

This session's opening prayer is in the form of a litany. Introduce the prayer with words such as these: "Each time we meet we will begin with prayer. Our prayers will be prompted by words from the Gospel of Mark. Our prayer today is in the form of a litany. I will speak a quote from Jesus, and then you will respond in unison with the words 'Help me, Lord Jesus.'" Repeat the response a couple of times, inviting the participants to repeat it with you.

Jesus said, "Follow me and I will make you fish for people" (1:17).

Jesus said, "Do not fear, only believe" (5:36).

Jesus said, "If any want to become my followers, let them deny themselves and take up their cross and follow me" (8:34).

Jesus said, "Whoever welcomes one such child in my name welcomes me" (9:37).

Jesus said, "You shall love the Lord your God with all your heart, and with all your soul, and with all your mind, and with all your strength. . . . [And] you shall love your neighbor as yourself" (12:30–31)

Building Community among the Participants

In this first session take a little time for persons to introduce themselves. Invite each person to state three things about himself or herself: name, a memory of a Sunday school or adult class attended in the past, and a favorite story about Jesus. Be sure to introduce yourself in this activity, perhaps even first in order to model what you have in mind. After all have introduced themselves, affirm what has been shared. Indicate that you have heard some wonderful memories and favorite Jesus stories and that this is a great foundation upon which to build a study of the Gospel of Mark.

Reviewing the Outline of Mark

Direct the group's attention to pages 50–53 in the Participant's Guide. This is the outline for the Gospel of Mark. Throughout the course it will be a helpful resource to return to frequently. Take a few minutes to skim it, calling attention to several important highlights:

- The Gospel is divided into four major parts or sections: (1) The Prologue: Before Jesus' Public Ministry, (2) The Powerful Christ, (3) The Suffering Christ, and (4) The Epilogue: The Empty Tomb, with parts 2 and 3 providing the bulk of the narrative.

- There are eighteen miracles in Mark, which are an important aspect of Mark's witness to Jesus.

- There are three phases to Jesus' ministry in part 2.

- Chapter 8 of Mark is not only the middle of the Gospel in terms of number of chapters, but it is also the middle in terms of the flow of the narrative.

- In part 3 there are three cycles focusing on Jesus' three passion predictions before entering Jerusalem.

- In part 3 when Jesus is in Jerusalem, five chapters are devoted to the last week of his life.

Defining Key Concepts

In the Participant's Guide we are introduced to five key concepts: the Synoptic Problem, gospel, canon, Markan priority, and oral tradition. Choose one of two ways to focus on these five key concepts. The first way is for you, the leader, to make a brief presentation of each of the five key concepts. To prepare for this presentation consult a Bible dictionary or other resource that will assist with background information on each concept. If you have a limited amount of time, this will probably be the best strategy.

The second way to work at defining these five concepts will take 15–20 minutes. Divide the group into five smaller groups with each group focusing on one concept. You will need to duplicate brief, relevant portions on each concept from several Bible study tools. It would be best if you could provide each group with photocopies of two or three brief essays that you can find in single-volume Bible dictionaries, study Bibles, and other similar resources (See the appendix on pages 114–16). It would be best to have two or three brief articles on each topic so that the persons in a group will have access to a variety of resources. After dividing into small groups and distributing the resources, give these directions:

- Divide the reading so that each person only needs to read one article.

- Underline the key phrases or sentences that help one to understand the key concept.

- Share the findings in your small group.

- Have one of the members of your group take a few notes to summarize the group's findings for sharing with the larger group.

- Reconvene as a total group so that each group can report its summary of the key concept.

Exploring "Immediately"

We have learned that the author of Mark uses the phrase "and immediately" as an abrupt transition between one event and another. Of the twenty-seven occurrences of the phrase in the NRSV translation of Mark, twenty of them appear in the first half of the Gospel. This exercise will help the group gain a glimpse of key events in the first half of Mark that are introduced with this phrase. The activity should take about ten minutes following these steps:

- Direct the group to turn to page 68 in the Leader's Guide (or to a handout you have prepared with the same information.)

- Assign one passage to each person in the group. If there are fewer than twenty persons, you don't need to assign all of the passages. If there are more than twenty persons, assign passages to pairs.

- Instruct the participants to read their verses and to notice two things: what precedes and what follows the "immediately" statement. If Mark's use of "immediately" is as a transition from one scene to another, what is the before and after in this portion of the narrative?

- Ask the participants to share, beginning with chapter 1, a brief summary of what is happening in the context of their passage.

- Conclude this activity with a question or two for discussion: What are some clues you discerned regarding the intent and the approach of the writer of the Gospel of Mark to presenting the work and witness of Jesus? What did you notice about the nature of Jesus' ministry?

Closing

The Gospel of Mark opens with these words: "The beginning of the good news of Jesus Christ, the Son of God" (1:1). Ask the participants to take a minute to think of those persons who have shared the good news of Jesus Christ with them personally: pastor, teacher, family member, friend, or someone else. In a few moments of silence invite them to reflect on memories associated with that person and to pray prayers of thanksgiving and intercession for her or him. After a minute or two of silence, ask group members to individually say aloud the name of the person they were remembering. After each person has spoken a name, invite all the group members to respond in unison, "Thank you, God, for this witness to your good news."

AFTER THE SESSION

Encourage the participants to read chapter 2 in the Participant's Guide and Mark 1:1–3:35 in preparation for the next class.

"Immediately" in the First Half of Mark's Gospel	
Mark 1:12	And the Spirit *immediately* drove him out into the wilderness.
Mark 1:18	And *immediately* they left their nets and followed him.
Mark 1:20	*Immediately* he called them; and they left their father Zebedee in the boat with the hired men, and followed him.
Mark 1:42	*Immediately* the leprosy left him, and he was made clean.
Mark 2:12	And he stood up, and *immediately* took the mat and went out before all of them; so that they were all amazed and glorified God, saying, "We have never seen anything like this!"
Mark 3:6	The Pharisees went out and *immediately* conspired with the Herodians against him, how to destroy him.
Mark 4:15	These are the ones on the path where the word is sown: when they hear, Satan *immediately* comes and takes away the word that is sown in them.
Mark 4:16	And these are the ones sown on rocky ground: when they hear the word, they *immediately* receive it with joy.
Mark 4:17	But they have no root, and endure only for a while; then, when trouble or persecution arises on account of the word, *immediately* they fall away.
Mark 5:2	And when he had stepped out of the boat, *immediately* a man out of the tombs with an unclean spirit met him.
Mark 5:29	*Immediately* her hemorrhage stopped; and she felt in her body that she was healed of her disease.
Mark 5:30	*Immediately* aware that power had gone forth from him, Jesus turned about in the crowd and said, "Who touched my clothes?"
Mark 5:42	And *immediately* the girl got up and began to walk about (she was twelve years of age). At this they were overcome with amazement.
Mark 6:25	*Immediately* she rushed back to the king and requested, "I want you to give me at once the head of John the Baptist on a platter."
Mark 6:27	*Immediately* the king sent a soldier of the guard with orders to bring John's head. He went and beheaded him in the prison.
Mark 6:45	*Immediately* he made his disciples get into the boat and go on ahead to the other side, to Bethsaida, while he dismissed the crowd.
Mark 6:50	But *immediately* he spoke to them and said, "Take heart, it is I; do not be afraid."
Mark 7:25	A woman whose little daughter had an unclean spirit *immediately* heard about him, and she came and bowed down at his feet.
Mark 7:35	And *immediately* his ears were opened, his tongue was released, and he spoke plainly.
Mark 8:10	And *immediately* he got into the boat with his disciples and went to the district of Dalmanutha.

The Beginning of the Gospel

A Study of Mark 1:1–3:35

BEFORE THE SESSION
Focus of the Session

The first thirteen verses of the first chapter of Mark's Gospel move from introduction to baptism to temptation in the wilderness. Then the first three chapters
move quickly from one action and miracle of Jesus to another. This session will
consider the actions of Jesus and the responses of various groups of persons to
those actions. It will also explore the cause and effect of Jesus' popularity.

Advance Preparation

- Read the first three chapters of the Gospel of Mark and
  then read chapter 2 in the Participant's Guide.

- If possible, use a study Bible or single-volume commentary to accompany your reading of Mark.

- Prepare and duplicate the two worksheets for this session.

- Provide extra Bibles for those who do not bring one.

- Print on a sheet of newsprint the words of the first stanza of "Christ of the Upward Way" to either sing or read for the closing.

Teaching Alternatives

The session plan that follows, like session 1, may have more activities than you have time available. If so, omit an activity or add a session.

DURING THE SESSION
Welcoming the Participants

Arrive at class early enough to set up the refreshments and to have everything ready before the first persons arrive. If you used name tags in the first session you will want to have them available again. It is possible that a new person or two will show up for this session. Be sure to welcome them warmly and assure them that even though they missed the first session you are sure they will catch on quickly and be able to participate easily.

Opening Prayer

After words of welcome and introductions of any new members of the group, invite the participants to join you in prayer. Offer the following prayer or one of your own creation.

> Loving God, we come to you in this time of study and reflection on your word for us in Mark's Gospel. We thank you for your faithful servants who have treasured your word so dearly as to be inspired to write, translate, interpret, and teach the words of Holy Scripture that reveal the Living Word, the Word made flesh in Jesus the Christ. By your Spirit, we pray that our hearts and minds will be open to hear you speak to us through the words of Mark and through the words we speak to one another. In the name of Jesus, our Lord, we pray. Amen.

Reviewing the Outline

Direct the group to pages 50–53 in the Participant's Guide. Look closely at sections I through IIA, the portion of Mark for our study in this session. Call attention to the brevity of the Prologue and to the fact that "The First Phase of Jesus' Public Ministry" features calling followers, preaching, healing, and controversy.

Comparing the Beginning of Mark with Other Gospels

Before beginning this activity, be sure everyone is aware of the following points:

- Mark was the earliest Gospel to be written.

- Matthew, Mark, and Luke are known as the Synoptic Gospels because of their similarities.

- Matthew and Luke include portions of Mark in their Gospels.

- Though narratives may appear in the same order and be similar in the three Gospels, there are, nevertheless, significant differences

This activity will help to identify the differences in the beginnings of Matthew, Mark, and Luke. There is a worksheet on page 75 to use for this activity. You may either make copies of the worksheet or duplicate it using the same format on a larger sheet of paper. Divide the larger group into smaller groups of three. Each person in each group will work with only one of the three Gospels. If the numbers do not come out even, two persons can focus on the same Gospel. Follow these steps:

- Assemble in small groups of three persons each.

- Distribute the worksheets, or have participants turn to page 75.

- Assign each person in the small group a different one of the three Gospels.

- Tell participants that each person is to answer the questions based on findings from his or her Gospel.

- After they have answered the questions, invite the three persons to compare notes with each other.

An alternative is to work as a whole group, inviting persons to share their findings one question at a time.

You should be able to accomplish the above steps in fifteen to twenty minutes. Afterward, engage the group members in a discussion using questions such as these:

- What are your impressions of what you have found as similarities and differences among the three Gospels?

- What do you notice as distinctive regarding the Gospel of Mark?

- In what ways does the narrative from the beginning of each Gospel through Jesus' temptation in the wilderness set the stage for presenting Jesus as the beloved Son of God?

Presenting the Call of the Disciples

Make a brief presentation on the subject of Jesus' calling of the disciples to accompany him. The focus on this part of the narrative is on the call of four fishermen (1:16–20) and Levi the tax collector (2:13–14). In your presentation be sure to include the following:

- Jesus was known as teacher and rabbi, and he gathered disciples to accompany him, as was the custom.

- The first four disciples called were fishermen: Simon (Peter), Andrew, James, and John.

- Notice the word "immediately" in the narrative. How quick was "immediately"?

- After Jesus called the four fishermen, the group went to Capernaum. There Jesus went to the synagogue and taught the people.

- Capernaum became the home base for Jesus while in Galilee, even though his hometown was Nazareth.

- While Jesus was walking by the Sea of Galilee he called Levi (also known as Matthew), a tax collector, while he was sitting in the tax booth. And, Levi, like the fishermen, followed Jesus "immediately."

- After calling Levi, Jesus joined his disciples, other tax collectors, and sinners for a meal at Levi's house.

- Jesus was criticized by the scribes of the Pharisees for eating with persons who were of questionable repute.

- Jesus responded with a statement about the nature of his ministry—to call sinners to repentance.

Comparing Jesus' Healing Miracles

In this first phase of Jesus' public ministry (1:21–3:35) there are five healing miracles. In this activity, participants will compare the five miracles in order to see the similarities and differences between them. Guide the group in the following steps, which should take no more than fifteen minutes:

- Divide the group into smaller groups of five persons each or into five small groups. If your group has fewer than ten members, they can work on the task as a whole group, one passage at a time.

- Direct the group to page 76 in the Leader's Guide for the worksheet "Comparing Five Healing Miracles of Jesus" or prepare and duplicate a worksheet following the same format to distribute to the group.

- You may find it helpful to prepare a large piece of newsprint with a similar format as the worksheet so that you can record the answers as they are given.

- Assign each person a different one of the five passages to read and several questions to answer.

- After participants have read their passages and answered their questions, have them share their answers with the other members of their group.

Following the sharing in the small groups, take a few minutes with the whole group to reflect on one or two questions, such as these:

- What insights have you gained regarding the nature of Jesus' ministry?

- What to you is the most surprising thing about this aspect of Jesus' ministry?

Reflecting on Affirmations and Criticisms of Jesus

In these first three chapters of Mark we see a variety of responses to the actions and teachings of Jesus: "his fame began to spread throughout . . . Galilee" (1:28), "the whole city was gathered around the door" (1:33), "people came to him from every quarter" (1:45), "they were all amazed and glorified God" (2:12), and five disciples followed him, immediately (1:18, 20; 2:14). These were the favorable responses. In addition, there were several responses that questioned or were critical of Jesus: "Why does he eat with tax collectors and sinners?" (2:16), "Look, why are they doing what is not lawful on the sabbath?" (2:24), "The Pharisees went out and immediately conspired with the Herodians against him, how to destroy him" (3:6), "People were saying, 'He has gone out of his mind'" (3:21), and "He has Beelzebul, and by the ruler of the demons he casts out demons" (3:22). Take a few minutes to guide the group in reflecting on these affirmations and criticisms. Look at each of the above passages and then respond to some or all of these questions:

- Who responds to Jesus positively? Why? How does Jesus respond?

- Who is critical of Jesus? Why? How does Jesus respond?

- What do these affirmations and criticisms of Jesus in the first three chapters of Mark tell us about the nature of Jesus' ministry?

- What do you think the writer of Mark is seeking to communicate about Jesus?

Closing

Bring closure to the session by praying or singing together the words of a familiar hymn, "Christ of the Upward Way":

> Christ of the upward way, My guide divine,
> Where you have set your feet, May I place mine;
> And move and march wherever You have trod,
> Keeping face forward up the hill of God.

AFTER THE SESSION

Encourage the participants to read chapter 3 in the Participant's Guide and Mark 4:1–7:37 as they are able in preparation for the next class.

Comparing the Beginnings of Matthew, Mark, and Luke

	Matthew	Mark	Luke
1. How many chapters and verses precede the baptism of Jesus?			
2. What are the key events in the narrative from the beginning of the Gospel up to Jesus' baptism?			
3. What are the unique features of the baptism-of-Jesus narrative?			
4. What do the voices from heaven and the cloud say?			
5. What is the number and order of the devil's temptations of Jesus?			
6. How does the narrative of the temptation of Jesus end?			

Comparing Five Healing Miracles of Jesus			
	What is the setting and who is present at the miracle?	Who is the recipient of the healing and what are the results?	What are the reactions to Jesus' miraculous act?
1. Exorcism in synagogue in Capernaum (1:21–28)			
2. Curing Simon's mother-in-law (1:29–31)			
3. Cleansing a leper (1:40–45)			
4. Healing a paralytic (2:1–12)			
5. Healing a man's withered hand on the Sabbath (3:1–6)			

Session Three

Jesus the Wonder Worker

A Study of Mark 4:1–7:37

BEFORE THE SESSION

Focus of the Session

This session will examine eight miracles of Jesus, one parable, and narratives describing his lack of success in Nazareth and his conflict with the religious authorities. There is a lot of material to cover in this session. You will lead the group in several engaging activities and a discussion guided by analytical questions that invite the participants to think and reflect on what they have read. You will not have time to deal with the narratives related to the mission of the Twelve and John the Baptist. A key question to focus on in this session is "What is the nature of this man from God who does such marvelous deeds and speaks with such authority?"

Advance Preparation

- Read Mark 4–7 and then read chapter 3 in the Participant's Guide.

- If possible, use a study Bible or single-volume commentary to accompany your reading of Mark.

- Provide extra Bibles for those who forget to bring one to class.

- Prepare your notes for the two brief presentations you will be making.

- Prepare the questions you will ask to guide discussion on the portions of Mark that will be explored in the activities for this session.

- Use a Bible dictionary, study Bible, or other resource to gather information to share related to the following topics: the messianic secret, the nature of parables, Pharisees, scribes, and Jewish traditions regarding eating.

DURING THE SESSION
Welcoming the Participants

Arrive at class early enough to set up the refreshments and to have everything ready before the first persons arrive. Ask the participants to sign in and make name tags for themselves. Greet each one by name and with a warm welcome. Check to see who needs to borrow a Bible. If anyone does, encourage him or her to bring a Bible to the next session. Give a copy of this course book to any participants who do not already have one.

Opening Prayer

After offering words of welcome and introductions of any who are present for the first time, invite the participants to join you in prayer. Introduce the prayer by stating that later in this session you will focus on Jesus teaching in the synagogue in Nazareth, his hometown. Jesus' teaching surprised the people who knew him well. No doubt he taught from God's word in the Law and the Prophets, and that word from God could be unsettling. The words of the opening prayer are from Psalm 146, which summarizes some of the teachings from

God's word. Invite the participants to turn to page 84 in the Leader's Guide. Divide the group in half, with one side reading the odd verses in plain text and the other side reading the verses in italics.

Reviewing Mark 4:1–7:37

Look at the outline of the Gospel of Mark on pages 50–53. Call attention to the movement of this portion of Mark from a discourse on parables, to four miracles (three healings and a nature miracle), to the commissioning of the Twelve, to the death of John the Baptist, to two miracles, to controversy with the Pharisees, and concluding with two more healing miracles. The purpose of this review is to help the participants gain an overall sense of the development of Jesus' ministry in these four chapters of Mark.

Explain to participants that they will not have time to explore in depth the more than a dozen narratives that are present in these four chapters but will focus on selected narratives either in small groups or as a whole class.

Reflecting on One Parable

Begin by making a brief presentation on the subject of parables in the Gospel of Mark. Use a commentary on Mark and/or notes from a study Bible to prepare your presentation. Be sure to include the following key points:

- Chapter 4 begins with Jesus teaching a large crowd. The crowd is so large that Jesus must sit in a boat, while the crowd sits or stands on the shore.

- One of the major teaching methods of Jesus was the use of parables.

- Parables are brief stories based on objects and experiences familiar to the listeners.

- The purpose of parables is to use concrete images to explain abstract concepts; for instance, comparing the kingdom of God to a mustard seed.

- Mark includes very few parables (4) compared to Matthew (15) and Luke (18).

- The parable of the Sower is found in all three Gospels, with some subtle differences in Luke compared to Matthew and Mark.

- In Mark, the parable of the Sower is presented in two parts; the first is the straightforward telling of the parable (4:3–9), followed by Jesus' explanation of it (4:10–20).

- The parable of the Sower is more like an allegory where the elements of the parable correspond to particular aspects in the narrative of the Gospel as a whole.

Read Mark 4:1–20, using the reading as formatted on page 85 of the Leader's Guide. First, determine who readers 1 and 2 will be, and then divide the class into four smaller groups. The two readers and four groups will read their respective lines. After the parable has been read, engage the class in a discussion using the following questions or those you have prepared:

- This is commonly known as the parable of the Sower. After reading the parable, do you think the emphasis is more on the sower, on the seeds, or on the soils? What might be another way of naming this parable?

- On page 22 of the Participant's Guide the author explains the allegorical connections to all the elements of the parable in terms of Jesus' day. What are some connections you would make between the four kinds of soil and life as we know it today?

- Jesus says, "To you has been given the secret of the kingdom of God, but for those outside, everything comes in parables" (4:11). Who are the ones to whom the secret is given? What is the secret? What do you think are the responsibilities of those who have the secret?

Connecting with Jesus' Miraculous Acts

Miracle narratives form the major part of these four chapters of Mark. Although there will not be time to go into all the details of each miracle, you can provide an opportunity for each member of the class to focus on one miracle. Direct the participants to turn to page 86 in the Leader's Guide, where there is a worksheet for this activity. The following points will be helpful as you lead the group through the process of reading and responding to these miracle narratives:

- Invite each person to choose one of the miracle narratives. If several people choose the same narrative, or if some narratives are not chosen, that is not a problem. Just be sure that there is a variety of narratives chosen.

- Review the directions printed on the worksheet to be sure that everyone understands what is expected.

- Emphasize that the retelling is not a test of memory but rather just a way for them to summarize the narrative they have read and thought about.

- After time for reading and reflecting (five to eight minutes), direct the participants to team up with one or two other persons who have chosen different narratives.

- Encourage the participants in their retelling of the narratives to talk about Jesus and the thoughts and feelings they have about him.

- Provide about five minutes for the pairs or small groups to retell their narratives.

When everyone has had a chance to share their narratives, call the group back for discussion of one question: What have you learned by putting yourselves into the role of someone who was present at one of Jesus' miraculous acts?

Presenting the Jesus-in-Nazareth Narrative

Mark's account of Jesus in Nazareth is very similar to the same narrative in Matthew but quite different from the way it is presented in Luke. It would be helpful to look at the Mark and Luke narratives side-by-side in order to identify their similarities and differences. Here are several points to make:

- Mark reports that on the Sabbath Jesus began to teach, whereas in Luke, the reading of a passage from the prophet Isaiah precedes Jesus' teaching.

- In Mark this account comes well into the public ministry of Jesus (Mark 6:1–6), whereas in Luke this event initiates Jesus' public ministry (Luke 4:16–30), for it occurs even before the call of the first disciples (Luke 5:1–11).

- In Mark the people question the source of Jesus' wisdom and deeds of power, whereas Luke says that at first the people "spoke well of him and were amazed at the gracious words that came from his mouth" (Luke 4:22).

- In Mark and Luke, Jesus speaks about prophets being without honor in their hometown.

- Mark refers to Jesus as "the son of Mary," and Luke refers to him as "Joseph's son."

- Mark reports that Jesus "was amazed at their [i.e., the hometown citizens'] unbelief" (6:6), while in Luke, Jesus refers to the acts of two prophets, Elijah and Elisha, which demonstrate God's grace for non-Israelites.

- In Mark, Jesus leaves to go to other villages to teach, but in Luke, Jesus is driven out of the village and threatened with harm, though he walks through the crowd unharmed.

Continue the presentation of the Jesus-in-Nazareth narrative by discussing these questions:

- If you had been a resident of Nazareth and active in the synagogue, what reaction might you have had to Jesus, your neighbor for thirty years or so?

- What do you think was the reason for the unbelief of the people of Nazareth?

- What are some circumstances today that might arouse similar responses on the part of people of our congregation or town?

Discussing the Tradition of the Elders

The concluding narrative for this session is found in Mark 7:1–23, where we find Jesus in conflict with the Pharisees and some of the scribes, who question Jesus regarding the behavior of his disciples. Make a brief presentation that covers key points such as these:

- Who were the Pharisees and scribes?

- What were the laws regarding ritual washing of hands the Pharisees were referring to?

- Explain what Jesus means when he says, "You abandon the commandment of God and hold to human tradition" (7:8).

- Call attention to the shift in the narrative where Jesus moves from speaking to the Pharisees (7:1–13), to speaking to the crowd (7:14–15), to speaking with the disciples (7:17–23). If anyone asks what happened to verse 16, point to the footnote that states, "Other ancient authorities add verse 16."

Conclude this presentation by discussing a question or two from the following, or questions you have prepared:

- What do you make of the different ways Jesus responds to the Pharisees, the crowd, and the disciples?

- What might be some examples today of abandoning the commandment of God and holding on to human traditions?

Closing

For a closing litany, invite the participants to complete a sentence that begins, "Jesus . . ." Give them about thirty seconds to complete the sentence either on paper or in thought. After a time of silence invite them to share their sentences one at a time. In response to each sentence that is shared invite the group to say together in unison, "O God, thank you for the powerful words and acts of Jesus." Have these words printed on a sheet of newsprint for all to see.

AFTER THE SESSION

Encourage the participants to read chapter 4 in the Participant's Guide and Mark 8:1–10:52 in preparation for the next class.

Opening Prayer: Psalm 146

Praise the LORD!
Praise the LORD, O my soul!
I will praise the LORD as long as I live;
I will sing praises to my God all my life long.

Do not put your trust in princes,
in mortals, in whom there is no help.
When their breath departs, they return to the earth;
on that very day their plans perish.

Happy are those whose help is the God of Jacob,
whose hope is in the LORD their God,
who made heaven and earth,
the sea, and all that is in them;
who keeps faith forever;
who executes justice for the oppressed;
who gives food to the hungry.

The LORD sets the prisoners free;
the LORD opens the eyes of the blind.
The LORD lifts up those who are bowed down;
the LORD loves the righteous.
The LORD watches over the strangers;
he upholds the orphan and the widow,
but the way of the wicked he brings to ruin.
The LORD will reign forever,
your God, O Zion, for all generations.
Praise the LORD!

The Parable of the Sower: Mark 4:1–20

Reader 1: Again [Jesus] began to teach beside the sea. Such a very large crowd gathered around him that he got into a boat on the sea and sat there, while the whole crowd was beside the sea on the land. He began to teach them many things in parables, and in his teaching he said to them: "Listen! A sower went out to sow.

Group 1: "And as he sowed, some seed fell on the path, and the birds came and ate it up.

Group 2: "Other seed fell on rocky ground, where it did not have much soil, and it sprang up quickly, since it had no depth of soil. And when the sun rose, it was scorched; and since it had no root, it withered away.

Group 3: "Other seed fell among thorns, and the thorns grew up and choked it, and it yielded no grain.

Group 4: "Other seed fell into good soil and brought forth grain, growing up and increasing and yielding thirty and sixty and a hundredfold."

Reader 2: And he said, "Let anyone with ears to hear listen!"

Reader 1: When he was alone, those who were around him along with the twelve asked him about the parables.

Reader 2: And he said to them, "To you has been given the secret of the kingdom of God, but for those outside, everything comes in parables; in order that 'they may indeed look, but not perceive, and may indeed listen, but not understand; so that they may not turn again and be forgiven.'"

Reader 1: And he said to them, "Do you not understand this parable? Then how will you understand all the parables?

Group 1: "The sower sows the word. These are the ones on the path where the word is sown: when they hear, Satan immediately comes and takes away the word that is sown in them.

Group 2: "And these are the ones sown on rocky ground: when they hear the word, they immediately receive it with joy. But they have no root, and endure only for a while; then, when trouble or persecution arises on account of the word, immediately they fall away.

Group 3: "And others are those sown among the thorns: these are the ones who hear the word, but the cares of the world, and the lure of wealth, and the desire for other things come in and choke the word, and it yields nothing.

Group 4: "And these are the ones sown on the good soil: they hear the word and accept it and bear fruit, thirty and sixty and a hundredfold."

Eight Miracles of Jesus in Mark 4–7

1. Choose one of the eight miracles below to be your focus.

Mark 4:35–41	Jesus quiets the storm
Mark 5:1–20	Jesus heals the Gerasene demoniac
Mark 5:21–24a, 35–43	Jesus heals Jairus's daughter
Mark 5:24b–34	Jesus heals the woman with a hemorrhage
Mark 6:30–44	Jesus feeds the five thousand
Mark 6:45–52	Jesus walks on water
Mark 7:24–30	Jesus heals the Syrophoenician woman's daughter
Mark 7:31–37	Jesus heals the deaf-mute

2. Read the miracle narrative and think about these four questions:

   What need or situation is presented to Jesus?

   How does Jesus respond to the need or situation?

   What is the response of the key character(s) in the narrative?

   What do you think is the person's or the crowd's understanding or impression of Jesus?

3. After reading and thinking about the miracle, imagine that you are in the crowd or one of the key characters in the narrative. Imagine that you observed or experienced this miracle.

4. When directed, meet up with one or two other members of the class who have focused on different miracles than you did.

5. Retell the miracle narrative from the perspective of the character you have imagined. Speak in the first person as if this is something you have experienced or observed.

Session Four

Jesus the Prophet

A Study of Mark 8:1–10:52

BEFORE THE SESSION
Focus of the Session

Yet again there is too much material from Mark to cover adequately in one session. This session will focus then on the transition from the first half of Mark, where Jesus teaches the crowds and heals many, to the second half, where Jesus points toward Jerusalem and his subsequent arrest, conviction, crucifixion, and resurrection. This session will emphasize the disciples' recognition of Jesus as Messiah, Jesus' three passion predictions, the narrative of the transfiguration, and Jesus' teaching his followers the meaning of discipleship.

Advance Preparation

• Read Mark 8–10 and then read chapter 4 in the Participant's Guide.

- You will find a commentary or study Bible to be helpful, especially for Peter's declaration of Jesus as the Messiah and for the transfiguration.

- Provide extra Bibles for those who do not bring one.

- If you can find one, display a map that will show the location of Caesarea Philippi.

- Prepare or review the questions you will ask to guide discussion.

- Outline your notes for a couple of presentations.

Teaching Alternatives

If there is too much to cover in this session, you will need to omit one or more activities. In any case, include the activities that focus on Peter's declaration of Jesus as Messiah, the passion prediction narratives, and the discussion on discipleship.

DURING THE SESSION
Welcoming the Participants

Arrive at class early enough to set up the refreshments and to have everything ready before the first persons arrive. Ask the participants to sign in and make name tags for themselves. Greet each one by name and with a warm welcome. Check to see who needs to borrow a Bible. If anyone does, encourage him or her to bring a Bible to the next session. Give a copy of this course book to any participants who do not already have one.

Opening Prayer

After words of welcome and introductions of any who are present for the first time, invite the participants to join in prayer. Offer the following prayer, or one you have created.

> Calling God, help us to hear your voice as you speak to us through your holy word.
> Surprising God, open our minds and hearts to the mysteries of your truth and power.
> Faithful God, we give you praise and thanksgiving for never giving up on us.

Compassionate God, reach out to us with the healing touch of your love and grace.

Transforming God, by your Spirit renew us to become the persons you created us to be.

Revealing God, prepare us to recognize your presence in our midst as we gather in your name. Amen.

Reviewing the Miracle of the Healing of a Blind Man

In this opening activity direct the participants to Mark 8:22–26 and to the section on the healing of the blind man at Bethsaida on pages 29–30 of the Participant's Guide. Guide the class through this passage and the comments in the Participant's Guide in order to emphasize the following points:

- This narrative is at the transition point between the first and second halves of Mark.

- The healing narrative is not included in Matthew and Luke.

- There are similarities between the healing of the blind man at Bethsaida and the deaf-mute in the previous chapter.

- Prior to this healing, Jesus' power has been unfailing.

- Only in this healing does Jesus have to try a second time in order to be completely successful.

- Look closely at 8:22–26 to notice the importance of Jesus' touching: "took him by the hand," "laid his hands on him," and "laid his hands on his eyes."

Conclude your review of this narrative with questions such as the following or ones you have created:

- What do you think is the significance of Mark's including this narrative and the report that Jesus had to try a second time to heal the man's blindness?

- Think of some times when your first efforts to accomplish something were not fully successful and with a second try you were successful. How important was it for you to make the second effort?

- What are some examples you can think of from your experience where there was "power" in the touch of one to another?

Exploring the Identity of Jesus as Messiah

New Testament scholars see the narrative of Peter's declaring Jesus as the Messiah (Mark 8:27–30) as the turning point of the Gospel. This narrative divides the Gospel into two parts: the first part features Jesus' miraculous deeds and teaching, and the second part focuses on Jesus' journey to Jerusalem and his passion. Begin by introducing the passage and asking the group to retell the narrative without looking at the text. After all or most of the narrative has been recalled, turn to the text and then summarize by commenting on the following:

- Where was the region of Caesarea Philippi? (If you have a large map, point out the location, which is in Galilee, north of the Sea of Galilee.)

- Why might Jesus have been identified as John the Baptist, Elijah, or one of the prophets?

- What is the significance of Peter's identifying Jesus as the Messiah?

- What kind of a messiah were the Jews expecting? (Look at pages 30–31 in the Participant's Guide for more information about the Jewish notion of messiah.)

- Why did Jesus frequently admonish the disciples not to tell anyone about what they experienced with or knew about him? (See also 1:34, 44; 3:12; 5:43; 7:36; 8:30; 9:30.)

After your review of the passage, guide the group in thinking about Jesus as the Messiah, or the Christ, for us today. With the following discussion, try to help the class members to relate the meaning of Jesus as Messiah to their personal faith journey. The discussion may be guided by questions such as these:

- Jesus is a familiar name for many people today. What are some impressions you think people today have of Jesus?

- In Jesus' day his identity was associated with one of the prophets. With whom or what is Jesus associated today?

- Jesus asks the disciples, "But who do you say that I am?" Write a sentence or two as your own answer to Jesus' question. (After a few minutes, invite the participants to share their answers.)

Interpreting the Transfiguration

The best way to deal with the narrative of Jesus' transfiguration is to spend some time with the passage and make reference to the information in the Participant's Guide on page 33. You could read the passage a verse at a time, followed by brief comments that could include these:

- Jesus took Peter, James, and John with him. They were also the ones who accompanied him to where Jairus's daughter lay gravely ill (5:37) and to the garden of Gethsemane (14:33). This suggests that these three disciples had a close relationship with Jesus.

- They went to a high mountain by themselves. This recalls God's appearance on a mountain to Moses (Exod. 19:20) and to Elijah (1 Kgs. 19:11). Also, in Mark, Jesus went to a high mountain when he named the twelve apostles (3:13).

- Commentary from *The New Interpreter's Study Bible* reads, "Some Jews believed that Moses, like Elijah (2 Kgs. 2:9–12), had not died but instead was taken directly up to heaven (Deut. 34:5–6). At any rate, both are still alive in the divine realm and can talk with Jesus."[1]

- Compare what was spoken by the voice from the cloud with what the voice from heaven said at Jesus' baptism (1:11).

- A cloud was a common element in appearances by God in other settings involving Moses (Exod. 24:15–18), Isaiah (Isa. 4:5), and Ezekiel (Ezek. 1:4).

- The voice said, "Listen to him," which may suggest that the disciples were to focus their attention on what Jesus would say to them and not so much on the wonder of the experience itself.

1. Mary Ann Tolbert, notes on the Gospel of Mark, in *The New Interpreter's Study Bible* (Nashville: Abingdon Press, 2003), 8:1825.

- Refer again to Jesus' admonition to the disciples not to tell anyone what they had seen.

Conclude your presentation with a question to discuss: What does this transfiguration narrative say to you about Jesus and his mission?

Comparing Jesus' Passion Predictions

In this section of Mark there are three occasions when Jesus speaks about what is going to happen to him. *Prior* to each prediction, Jesus has a significant encounter with his disciples or other individuals. *After* each prediction, Jesus teaches something about the meaning of discipleship and what is expected of those who would follow him. Guide the class through the following activities:

- Direct the participants to page 94 of the Leader's Guide, where they will find the worksheet "Comparing Jesus' Three Passion Predictions."

- Form small groups of three persons each. (It is OK if there is an extra person in some groups, which means that two persons will be working with the same passage.)

- Each person is to focus on one passage and to answer the four questions according to that passage.

- After the participants have finished reading and answering the questions, provide time for them to compare notes with one another.

- Conclude by calling the group together and asking a summarizing question: What insights came to you as you read your passage and then compared your findings with the other two persons? Or move directly to discussing the questions in the next activity below.

Thinking about Discipleship

Question 4 on the worksheet of the previous activity leads the participants in summarizing what Jesus had to say about discipleship. In addition to what was found in the three passages, look at 10:13–16, where Jesus says, "Whoever does not receive the kingdom of God as a little child will never enter it." With this passage and the other teachings about discipleship, spend some time discussing a few open-ended questions:

- How would you summarize what Jesus taught his followers about discipleship?

- What are some questions you have about what Jesus requires of those who would follow him?

- To what extent are Jesus' expectations of his followers realistic or unrealistic in the twenty-first century?

- What are some other teachings of Jesus in Mark or the other Gospels that also describe what is expected of Jesus' followers?

- If you were to attempt to live according to what Jesus expects of his followers, which of his teachings would be the most challenging or difficult?

Closing

One of the featured concepts in this session is Jesus' teaching about the meaning of discipleship. Direct the participants to the "Litany of Discipleship" on page 95 in the Leader's Guide. Ask individuals in the group to take turns reading those statements identified as "One."

AFTER THE SESSION

Encourage the participants to read chapter 5 in the Participant's Guide and Mark 11:1–14:72 in preparation for the next session.

Comparing Jesus' Three Passion Predictions			
	Mark 8:31–33	Mark 9:30–32	Mark 10:32–34
1. What is featured in the narrative that *precedes* this passage?			
2. What does Jesus say will happen to him?			
3. What is featured in the narrative that *follows* this passage?			
4. What does Jesus teach about discipleship in the passage following his prediction?			

Litany of Discipleship

One: Jesus said, "If any want to become my followers, let them deny themselves and take up their cross and follow me" (8:34).

All: *O God, we do want to follow Jesus, but we are not sure about what it means to pick up a cross. Show us the crosses we are to bear and help us to do so, we pray.*

One: Jesus said, "Those who want to save their life will lose it, and those who lose their life for my sake, and for the sake of the gospel, will save it" (8:35).

All: *Teach us, Holy God, what it means to lose our life for Jesus' sake and for the gospel.*

One: Jesus said, "Whoever wants to be first must be last of all and servant of all" (9:35).

All: *Merciful God, our nature is to want to be first. May we learn from Jesus what it means to humble ourselves as he did and to be a servant of others in his name.*

One: Jesus said, "Whoever welcomes one such child in my name welcomes me, and whoever welcomes me welcomes not me but the one who sent me" (9:37).

All: *Loving God, enable us to extend hospitality to the overlooked and marginalized ones in our communities who need to be included as part of your larger family.*

One: Jesus said, "Let the little children come to me; do not stop them; for it is to such as these that the kingdom of God belongs. Truly I tell you, whoever does not receive the kingdom of God as a little child will never enter it" (10:14b–15).

All: *O God, remind me what it means to be childlike and to be open to the joy, the challenges, and the surprises that accompany being citizens of your kingdom.*

One: Jesus said, "Go; your faith has made you well" (10:52).

All: *We thank you, God, for calling us to follow Jesus and for sending us out to be witnesses to the truth and love we know in him. Amen.*

Session Five

The End of Jesus' Public Ministry

A Study of Mark 11:1–14:72

BEFORE THE SESSION
Focus of the Session

This session, focused on chapters 11–14, moves from Jesus' entrance into Jerusalem through many episodes in the final week of his life, concluding with the account of Peter's denying Jesus three times. It will lead participants to make connections between some Old Testament passages and the events recorded in Mark, explore several difficult passages, and identify with persons involved in important events of Jesus' last days.

Advance Preparation

- Read Mark 11–14 and then read chapter 5 in the Participant's Guide.

- You will find using a commentary or study Bible to be helpful, especially related to chapter 13, the "Little Apocalypse."

- Gather information from a Bible dictionary or study Bible on several topics: Pharisees, Herodians, chief priests, scribes, and elders.

- Provide extra Bibles for those who do not bring one.

- Prepare or review the questions you will ask.

- Outline your notes for a couple of presentations.

Teaching Alternatives

If there is too much to cover in this session plan, omit one or more activities. The activities that you might decide to omit from the plans for your session are "Interpreting a Curse and a Parable" and "Interpreting the 'Little Apocalypse.'" In order to save a little time, you might also consider doing the "Exploring Important Questions" activity as a whole group, one passage at a time, rather than in small groups.

DURING THE SESSION
Welcoming the Participants

Arrive at class early enough to set up the refreshments and to have everything ready before the first persons arrive. Ask the participants to sign in and make name tags for themselves. Greet each one by name and with a warm welcome. Check to see who needs to borrow a Bible. If anyone does, encourage him or her to bring a Bible to the next session. Give a copy of this course book to any participants who do not already have one.

Opening Prayer

After words of welcome, invite the participants to join you in prayer. This session's opening prayer is in the form of a litany. Introduce the prayer by stating that in chapters 11–14 there are several sayings of Jesus that will prompt our prayers. (The words of Jesus are presented below.) After each saying the group is to respond in unison, "O God, help me to understand these words of Jesus."

Repeat the response a couple of times, inviting the participants to repeat it with you. Or write the response on a sheet of newsprint for all to see.

> Jesus quoted the prophet Isaiah, "My house shall be called a house of prayer for all the nations" (11:17).

> Jesus said, "Whenever you stand praying, forgive, if you have anything against anyone; so that your Father in heaven may also forgive you your trespasses" (11:25).

> Jesus said, "Give to the emperor the things that are the emperor's, and to God the things that are God's" (12:17).

> Jesus said, "You shall love the Lord your God with all your heart, and with all your soul, and with all your mind, and with all your strength" (12:30).

> Jesus said, "You shall love your neighbor as yourself" (12:31).

> Jesus said, "Truly I tell you, this poor widow has put in more than all those who are contributing to the treasury. . . . She out of her poverty has put in everything she had" (12:43–44).

> Jesus said, "Heaven and earth will pass away, but my words will not pass away" (13:31).

> After breaking a loaf of bread and sharing a cup, Jesus said, "Take; this is my body" and "This is my blood of the covenant, which is poured out for many" (14:22, 24).

Connecting with Old Testament Passages

In the narratives of Jesus' entry into Jerusalem, his cursing of the fig tree, and his cleansing of the temple there are a number of actions and objects that have direct or indirect connections to passages in the Hebrew Scriptures of Jesus' day—what we know as the Old Testament. There are three steps to take in leading this activity:

1. Introduce the activity by sharing that the writer of the Gospel of Mark was familiar with the writings of the Law, the Prophets, and the Psalms. In addition, he is attuned to the marvelous deeds of God for the deliverance of the people of the covenant throughout their long history. With the Hebrew Scriptures, our Old Testament, as a backdrop for Mark's writing, it is not surprising that he makes a number of con-

nections between those Scriptures, especially the Prophets, and the actions and teachings of Jesus in these last days of his life.

2. Guide the group in reading the Mark and Old Testament passages using the script on pages 103–4, "Connecting with Old Testament Passages." Divide the group in half, with one half reading the Mark passages and the other half the Old Testament passages. It may be more dramatic to arrange for the two halves of the class to stand and face each other as they do the reading.

3. After the reading, engage the group in a discussion using questions such as the following, or ones that you will create:

   • What are some thoughts, questions, or impressions you have regarding the suggested connections between Mark and the Old Testament passages?

   • How would you describe Jesus' words and actions in these narratives?

   • Putting yourself in the place of the chief priests and scribes, what are some thoughts and impressions you would have had regarding Jesus?

   • What are some connections you might make between religious authority and the threats to that authority in Jesus' day, as well as religious authority and the need for reform in our day?

Interpreting a Curse and a Parable

The two passages to interpret in this activity are the curse of the fig tree (11:12–14, 20–26) and the parable of the Wicked Tenants (12:1–12). Perhaps the best way to deal with these two passages is to make a brief presentation. Review the material in the Participant's Guide (pages 38–39) and notes in a study Bible and/or a commentary on Mark. Some things to do and key points to make include the following:

   • Invite two readers to read the passage aloud, with reader 1 taking 11:12–14 and 11:20–26 and reader 2 taking 11:15–19. This is a good way to show Mark's bracketing device.

- Mark's focus on the fig tree is a literary device bracketing the narrative of Jesus' driving the money changers out of the temple in order to show that the temple is no longer fulfilling its purpose, just as a fig tree without fruit is not fulfilling its purpose.

- Was cursing the fig tree an abuse of power on the part of Jesus, or was it more likely a symbolic act that showed his criticism of the way in which the temple had become "a den of robbers"?

- The purpose of the temple was to be a place of prayer. Jesus offers a brief teaching on the importance of prayer: how to pray, what to pray for, and what to expect from prayer.

- Ask the same two readers to read the following passages: reader 1, 11:27–33 and 12:13–17, reader 2, 12:1–12.

- The parable of the Wicked Tenants is bracketed by episodes of Jesus being questioned, first by the chief priests, the scribes, and the elders, and afterward by the Pharisees and Herodians. They challenge the source of Jesus' authority and the way he interprets the law.

- Describe who the priests, scribes, elders, Pharisees, and Herodians were.

- Call attention to the characters in the parable as representative of what was happening in the life of God's people: planter or owner of the vineyard = God, vineyard/tenants = Israel, the slaves = the prophets, and beloved son = Jesus.

- In this parable Jesus is describing what is going to happen to him in his suffering and death.

Conclude this section by discussing a question or two such as these: What are some of your observations or insights regarding Jesus as reflected in these passages compared to what we have learned about Jesus previous to this in Mark? What questions are raised in your mind regarding the intentions and actions of Jesus?

Exploring Important Questions

In Mark 11 and 12 there are four questions raised regarding Jesus' authority and/or his interpretation of the religious traditions of his people. The activity sheet for this activity is found on page 105. Divide the class into four small groups and assign each group a different one of the four passages. Everyone is to read their assigned passage and then answer in their group the three questions based on their passage. After about ten minutes call the small groups back and ask a representative from each to share his or her small group's answers to the three questions. Then guide the entire group in a brief discussion using several of the questions suggested below or questions you have planned.

- How would you describe the motivations of those who questioned Jesus?

- What do you think of the way Jesus responded to the questioners?

- Which of Jesus' responses do you think was most troublesome to the questioners?

- To what extent do you think Jesus' responses led to his suffering and death?

Interpreting the "Little Apocalypse"

Mark 13 is widely referred to as the "Little Apocalypse." This is a difficult passage, and the class will need some assistance in trying to interpret what Mark, through the words of Jesus, means for his readers to understand. References to page 40 in the Participant's Guide, notes in a study Bible, and a commentary on Mark will be very helpful. You will need to decide whether or not there is enough time to work with this passage and if you feel sufficiently prepared to help participants in understanding it.

Retelling the Events in Jesus' Last Days

There are seven episodes in the fourteenth chapter of Mark. Assign a different episode to each person. (If there are fewer than seven persons in your class, just assign selected passages. If there are more than seven, assign the same passage to two or more persons.)

14:3–9   Anointing at Bethany

14:12–25 Passover meal and Last Supper

14:26–31 Peter's denial predicted

14:32–42 Jesus prays in Gethsemane

14:10–11, 43–52   Betrayal and arrest of Jesus

14:53–65 Jesus before the council

14:66–72 Peter denies Jesus

Ask each person to read his or her passage and to imagine himself or herself as one of the key characters. Alert participants that after a few minutes they will be invited to retell the event in the words of the character they chose. (Where two persons have read the same passage, ask them to each retell just a part of the narrative.) After this retelling, ask the group to reflect on one or more of these questions:

- How did it feel to be part of the story?

- What are some of your impressions of Jesus from the perspective of the person you identified with?

- What relevance is there to these views of Jesus to faith and life today?

Closing

Invite the participants to form a circle, and then close by praying together in unison the Lord's Prayer.

AFTER THE SESSION

Encourage the participants to read chapter 6 in the Participant's Guide and Mark 15:1–16:8 in preparation for the next session.

Connecting with Old Testament Passages	
Mark	When they were approaching Jerusalem, at Bethphage and Bethany, near the Mount of Olives, he sent two of his disciples and said to them, "Go into the village ahead of you, and immediately as you enter it, you will find tied there a colt that has never been ridden; untie it and bring it" (11:1–2).
Zechariah	*Rejoice greatly, O daughter Zion! Shout aloud, O daughter Jerusalem! Lo, your king comes to you; triumphant and victorious is he, humble and riding on a donkey* (Zech. 9:9).
Mark	Many people spread their cloaks on the road, and others spread leafy branches that they had cut in the fields (11:8).
2 Kings	*"'Thus says the LORD, I anoint you king over Israel.'" Then hurriedly they all took their cloaks and spread them for him on the bare steps; and they blew the trumpet, and proclaimed, "Jehu is king"* (2 Kgs. 9:12b–13)
Mark	Then those who went ahead and those who followed were shouting, "Hosanna! Blessed is the one who comes in the name of the Lord! Blessed is the coming kingdom of our ancestor David! Hosanna in the highest heaven!" (11:9–10).
Psalmist	*Blessed is the one who comes in the name of the LORD. We bless you from the house of the LORD. The LORD is God, and he has given us light. Bind the festal procession with branches, up to the horns of the altar* (Ps. 118:26–27).
Mark	On the following day, when they came from Bethany, he was hungry. Seeing in the distance a fig tree in leaf, he went to see whether perhaps he would find anything on it. When he came to it, he found nothing but leaves, for it was not the season for figs. He said to it, "May no one ever eat fruit from you again." And his disciples heard it (11:12–14).
Prophets	*Like grapes in the wilderness, I found Israel. Like the first fruit on the fig tree, in its first season, I saw your ancestors* (Hos. 9:10). *The voice of the LORD cries to the city. . . . Woe is me! For I have become like one who, after the summer fruit has been gathered, after the vintage has been gleaned, finds no cluster to eat; there is no first-ripe fig for which I hunger. The faithful have disappeared from the land, and there is no one left who is upright* (Mic. 6:9a, 7:1–2b).

Connecting with Old Testament Passages *(continued)*	
Mark	Then they came to Jerusalem. And he entered the temple and began to drive out those who were selling and those who were buying in the temple, and he overturned the tables of the money changers and the seats of those who sold doves; and he would not allow anyone to carry anything through the temple. He was teaching and saying, "Is it not written, 'My house shall be called a house of prayer for all the nations'? But you have made it a den of robbers" (11:15–17).
Prophets	*All who keep the sabbath, and do not profane it, and hold fast my covenant—these I will bring to my holy mountain, and make them joyful in my house of prayer; their burnt offerings and their sacrifices will be accepted on my altar; for my house shall be called a house of prayer for all peoples* (Isa. 56:6b–7). *Has this house, which is called by my name, become a den of robbers in your sight? You know, I too am watching, says the* LORD (Jer. 7:11).
Mark	And when the chief priests and the scribes heard it, they kept looking for a way to kill him; for they were afraid of him, because the whole crowd was spellbound by his teaching. And when evening came, Jesus and his disciples went out of the city (11:18–19).

Exploring Important Questions			
	Who questions Jesus?	What is the question or the issue?	How does Jesus respond?
1. Mark 11:27–33 (a question of Jesus' authority in general)			
2. Mark 12:13–17 (a question regarding paying taxes)			
3. Mark 12:18–27 (a question regarding the resurrection)			
4. Mark 12:28–34 (a question regarding the commandments)			

Session Six

The End of the Gospel?

A Study of Mark 15:1–16:8

BEFORE THE SESSION

Focus of the Session

In this session our study of the Gospel of Mark comes to a close. In between opening and closing prayers, the focus of this session is upon three major topics: the crucifixion of Jesus in Mark 15, the empty tomb in Mark 16, and the experience of the class throughout the study.

Advance Preparation

- Read Mark 15–16 and then read chapter 6 in the Participant's Guide.

- Be sure you have reviewed the directions for the opening prayer activity focusing on expressions of trust in Psalms so that you can lead the activity confidently.

- If you choose to summarize the ten key characters of Mark 15 by sharing the passages and a few comments related to each, you will need to prepare an outline of notes for your comments.

- If you choose to engage the participants in exploring the ten key characters, you will need to prepare resource sheets related to each character by duplicating brief articles from a Bible dictionary or comments from a Bible commentary or study Bible.

- In order to do the "Reflecting on the Crucifixion" activity you will need to gather a collection of appropriate visuals depicting the events and characters presented in Mark 15. There are several potential sources for obtaining such visuals. The most accessible source is the church school collection of teaching prints that have accumulated over the years. There are also many sources on the Internet of royalty-free visuals of paintings, sculpture, and stained glass images. Finally, many books have art prints and visual images related to the life of Christ. If you use this type of resource you will not be able to mount the visuals on a bulletin board, but they could still serve a useful purpose.

- Prepare or review the questions you will ask to guide discussion.

- For the "Comparing Four Empty-Tomb Narratives" activity, prepare on a sheet of newsprint a large grid similar to the one on page 113 of the Leader's Guide. This will help you to record and make visible the responses of the four small groups. In addition, those who want to record the answers on the resource sheet in their books will be able to follow along easily.

- Think through the process and the questions you want to use to guide the class in evaluating their experience with this course.

- Print out on a sheet of newsprint the unison response for the closing litany prayer.

DURING THE SESSION
Opening Prayer

Throughout the Gospel of Mark, Jesus is depicted as one who trusts God completely and calls his followers to trust God. In the spirit of trusting God, this opening prayer invites the participants to spend a few minutes with expressions of trust in the book of Psalms. The activity will take between eight and ten minutes with the following directions:

- Ask the participants to turn to the book of Psalms and open to a random page.

- Invite them to skim some psalms forward or backward from the place where they opened the book. They are to look for a few verses that express the psalmist's trust, confidence, faith, or hope in God.

- Explain that they will have just four or five minutes for this process but that you are sure they will find appropriate verses.

- Invite class members to read the verses they selected as their prayers. After every verse the whole group will respond in unison, "God's steadfast love endures forever."

After the sharing of verses of trust in God and responding in unison, make a comment such as this: "In our study today we will encounter many unpleasant images of abandonment, violence, and death. However, we need to keep in mind the trust in God that Jesus had throughout his ministry and the hope he promised on several occasions that the Son of Man would rise from death on the third day. Jesus calls us to have the same trust, confidence, faith, and hope in God that he had."

Identifying the Key Characters

In Mark 15 there are a number of key characters involved in the dramatic events of the last day of Jesus' life. It is important to focus on these characters and their roles in what happened to Jesus. The key characters include:

Chief priests (15:1–5)

Elders and scribes (15:1–6)

Pilate (15:1–5)

Barabbas (15:6–15)

Cohort of soldiers (15:16–20)

Simon of Cyrene (15:21–24)

Mary Magdalene (15:40–41, 47)

Mary the mother of James (15:40–41, 47)

Salome (15:40–41)

Joseph of Arimathea (15:42–47)

There are two ways of reviewing these ten different characters. One is to present a brief description of each and then to look at the key passages where they are mentioned. The second is to duplicate short articles from a single-volume Bible dictionary and/or notes from a commentary for each of the characters, plus the passages where they are mentioned. Small groups of two or three participants can each focus on one of the characters in order to prepare a brief report describing who they are and what their roles were in Jesus' trial, suffering, and crucifixion. This second approach will take more time than the first.

Two questions should be asked regarding each of the key characters:

- What was the character's role in the narrative?

- How did the person or persons respond to Jesus, if there was a response?

Conclude by commenting that nowhere in chapter 15 is there any mention of the twelve disciples either as a group or individually. Ask participants why they think that is the case.

Reflecting on the Crucifixion

The above activity will have provided an overview of chapter 15 and its account of the crucifixion of Jesus. There is another way to reflect on those events using some visual resources. The goal is to gather a dozen or more visual images of the events of Jesus' crucifixion as presented in Mark 15. See the "Advance Preparation" section for some suggestions of how you might be able to obtain a variety of visual images for the class members to use in their reflecting on the crucifixion.

There are several alternative ways in which you could lead the class. The way you choose will be determined by several factors: the number of visuals you have available, the amount of time you have, the number of participants in the class, and your comfort level in leading the activity.

Option 1: Invite each class member to select a different one of the several visuals you provided to be the focus of his or her attention. (Be sure to provide more visuals than there are participants so that the last person who chooses will still have several from which to choose.) After each person has chosen a visual, lead a guided meditation. Ask several prompting questions followed by a brief silence to guide each participant to reflect on his or her visual. After a few minutes, break the silence and ask the participants to share why they chose the prints they did and what insights came to them through their meditation on the visual.

Option 2: Prepare ahead of time printed cards with names of the ten key characters that were identified in the previous activity. Post the cards in a row across the top of a bulletin board, and then as a group select from among the available visuals those that can be placed under their respective names. Give participants blank 3x5 cards to write captions for posting beside or under their respective visuals. Conclude by standing in front of the display of visuals and captions to share observations with one another.

Option 3: If in the previous activity you chose to present information about the ten key characters, in this option distribute visuals illustrating each of the ten characters (or as many of the characters as you have visuals to represent) to individuals or small groups. Ask them to arrange themselves in the order of the sequence of events in Mark 15 and then for each to share an interpretation of the passage and its related visual.

No matter which option you choose, conclude by discussing one question: What insights have come to you regarding the nature and the purpose of the crucifixion of Jesus?

Comparing Four Empty-Tomb Narratives

In page 48 of the Participant's Guide, the point is made that in the earliest manuscript of the Gospel of Mark, chapter 16 ends at verse 8, with verses 9 to 20 added at a later time. Lead the group in comparing Mark's account of the empty tomb with the accounts of the other three Gospels. (Compare just the narratives related to the empty tomb, not the additional resurrection appearance narratives.) Follow these directions for guiding this activity:

- Use the worksheet provided on page 113 in the Leader's Guide.

- Form four small groups of equal size and assign each group a different one of the four Gospels.

- Tell the members of each small group to read their assigned passage and then answer the six questions based on their Gospel's account.

- After the small groups have answered the questions, call everyone back to the large group and deal with one question at a time by presenting the answer from each of the Gospels. (You may want to prepare a large grid on a sheet of newsprint or on a marking board in order to record the answers to each question for each Gospel.)

After all of the answers have been presented by each of the groups, spend a few minutes discussing together one or more of the following questions, or questions you have created.

- When you compare the answers for Mark with the other three Gospels, what do you notice as the major differences between Mark and the others?

- What do you see as the common witness of all four Gospels?

- What do you make of the differences in the responses of those who went to the empty tomb?

- What does that suggest to you regarding responses we might make today to the resurrection of Jesus the Christ?

- Which of the empty-tomb narratives do you prefer? Why?

Evaluating the Course

Introduce this evaluation by telling the group something like this: "We have spent a number of weeks together studying the Gospel of Mark. We have read the Participant's Guide and many passages in Mark, we have participated in a variety of activities together, and we have discussed many questions. It is impossible to remember all we have said and done together, but I am sure there are some things that are memorable from your study." Then wrap up the course by leading the class in discussion of as many of the following questions as you have time for.

- Of all the activities we did together, which ones were the most interesting, challenging, or helpful for you?

- What are some suggestions you would make regarding a future study like this one?

- What are some questions that have been provoked in your mind about the life and ministry of Jesus from the perspective of Mark's Gospel?

- The title of this session, "The End of the Gospel?" ends with a question mark. What do you think the author intended by that title?

- What are some new insights you have gained as a result of this study?

- How has this study contributed to your personal faith journey?

- Where do you hope this study will lead you, our group, and/or our church?

Closing

Make a transition from the above discussion to this closing activity by asking the class members to complete this sentence: "God acted in Jesus the Christ to . . ." After a minute or two, invite the class members to share their completed sentences. In response to each person's sentence lead the whole group to respond in unison with "Redeemer God, thank you for what you have revealed to us in Jesus." (Print this response on a sheet of newsprint or marking board for all to see.)

Conclude this session and the course by singing together the familiar Easter hymn "Jesus Christ Is Risen Today" or reading the words in unison.

Comparing Four Empty-Tomb Narratives				
	Matthew 28:1–10	**Mark 16:1–8**	**Luke 24:1–12**	**John 20:1–10**
1. Who went to the tomb?				
2. When did they go to the tomb?				
3. What did they find? Whom did they encounter?				
4. What was said to them?				
5. How did they respond emotionally?				
6. What did they do?				

Appendix

Commentaries on Mark

Achtemeier, Paul J. *Mark*. 2nd ed. Proclamation Commentaries. Philadelphia: Fortress Press, 1986.

Boring, Eugene M. *Mark: A Commentary*. New Testament Library. Louisville, KY: Westminster John Knox Press, 2006.

Juel, Donald H. *The Gospel of Mark*. Interpreting Biblical Texts. Nashville: Abingdon Press, 1999.

———. *Mark*. Augsburg Commentary on the New Testament. Minneapolis: Augsburg Press, 1990.

Perkins, Pheme. "Introduction, Commentary, and Reflections on Mark." Pages 507–734 in *The New Interpreter's Bible*, vol. 8. Edited by Leander Keck. Nashville: Abingdon Press, 1995.

Rhoads, David, and Donald Mitchie. *Mark as Story*. Philadelphia: Fortress Press, 1982.

Tolbert, Mary Ann. *Sowing the Gospel: Mark's World in Literary-Historical Perspective*. Minneapolis: Fortress Press, 1989.

Williamson, Lamar. *Mark*. Atlanta: John Knox Press, 1983.

Bible Study Aids

Achtemeier, Paul J., gen. ed. *The HarperCollins Bible Dictionary*. San Francisco: HarperCollins Publishers in consultation with the Society of Biblical Literature, 1996.

Mays, James L., gen. ed. *The HarperCollins Bible Commentary*. Rev. ed. San Francisco: HarperCollins Publishers in consultation with the Society of Biblical Literature, 2000.

Throckmorton, Burton H., ed. *Gospel Parallels: A Comparison of the Synoptic Gospels*. 5th ed. Nashville: Thomas Nelson, 1992.

Study Bibles

The Access Bible (NRSV). New York: Oxford University Press, 1999.

> Features include introductory articles for each book of the Bible; sidebar essays, maps, and charts in places appropriate to the text; section-by-section commentaries on the text; a glossary; a brief concordance; and a section of Bible maps in color.

The Discipleship Study Bible with Apocrypha (NRSV). Louisville, KY: Westminster John Knox Press, 2008.

> Features include introductory articles for each book of the Bible, study notes for key portions of each chapter of the Bible, a concise concordance, and helpful maps.

The Learning Bible (CEV). New York: American Bible Society, 2000.

> Features include introductory articles and outlines for each book of the Bible; fifteen background articles and over one hundred mini-articles; charts and timelines; a mini-atlas; notes on biblical texts in six categories, each identified by a different color and symbol (geography; people and nations; objects, plants, and animals; ideas and concepts; history and culture; and cross-references); and hundreds of illustrations, photographs, and diagrams in color.

The New Interpreter's Study Bible with Apocrypha (NRSV). Nashville: Abingdon Press, 2003.

> Features include introductory articles for each book of the Bible, extensive textual notes, many excursus essays, a helpful glossary, general articles related to biblical authority and interpretation, and colorful maps.

The NIV Study Bible. Grand Rapids: Zondervan, 1985.

> Features include introductory articles and outlines for each book of the Bible; extensive notes for explanation and interpretation of the biblical text on each page; helpful charts, maps, and diagrams within the biblical text; an index to subjects; a concise concordance; and a collection of maps in color.

Introductory Works on the Synoptic Gospels

Nickel, Keith F. *The Synoptic Gospels: An Introduction*. Rev. and expanded ed. Louisville: Westminster John Knox Press, 2001.

Perkins, Pheme. *Introduction to the Synoptic Gospels.* Grand Rapids: Wm. B. Eerdmans Publishing Co., 2007.

Works on the Death of Jesus

Brown, Raymond E. *The Death of the Messiah: From Gethsemane to the Grave.* 2 vols. Anchor Bible Reference Library. New York: Doubleday, 1994.

Crossan, John Dominic. *Who Killed Jesus? Exposing the Roots of Anti-Semitism in the Gospel Story of the Death of Jesus.* San Francisco: HarperCollins, 1995.

Sloyan, Gerard S. *The Crucifixion of Jesus: History, Myth, Faith.* Minneapolis: Fortress Press, 1995.

Strange, James F. "Crucifixion, Method of." Pages 199–200 in *The Interpreter's Dictionary of the Bible.* Supplementary vol. Edited by Keith Crim. Nashville: Abingdon Press, 1976.

green press
INITIATIVE

Presbyterian Publishing is committed to preserving ancient forests and natural resources. We elected to print this title on 30% post consumer recycled paper, processed chlorine free. As a result, for this printing, we have saved:

12 Trees (40' tall and 6-8" diameter)
4 Million BTUs of Total Energy
1,179 Pounds of Greenhouse Gases
5,676 Gallons of Wastewater
345 Pounds of Solid Waste

Presbyterian Publishing made this paper choice because our printer, Thomson-Shore, Inc., is a member of Green Press Initiative, a nonprofit program dedicated to supporting authors, publishers, and suppliers in their efforts to reduce their use of fiber obtained from endangered forests.

For more information, visit www.greenpressinitiative.org

Environmental impact estimates were made using the Environmental Defense Paper Calculator. For more information visit: www.edf.org/papercalculator